Halloween Cookbook

A HOLIDAY COOKBOOK

Halloween Cookbook

by Susan Purdy

FRANKLIN WATTS I NEW YORK I LONDON I 1977

Library of Congress Cataloging in Publication Data

Purdy, Susan Gold
  Halloween cookbook.

  (A Holiday cookbook)
  Includes index.
  SUMMARY: Recipes with metric equivalents for
Halloween and the fall, with ideas for edible
decorations and tips on measurements and basic
cooking skills.
  1. Cookery—Juvenile literature. 2. Halloween—
Juvenile literature. [1. Cookery. 2. Halloween]
I. Title.
TX652.5.P87   641.5′68   77-6428
ISBN 0-531-01320-0
ISBN 0-531-01340-5 pbk.

For Tabitha

203163

For help in the development and testing of these recipes, I would like to thank Sara Jane Chelminski, Barbara Cover, Joan Sommer, Elizabeth Mac-Donald, Barbara Redd, Ruth Joan Dobsevage, and Beatrice and Jordan Joslin. For advice on the use of the metric system, I am indebted to Mrs. Daisy Brannick; Dr. Sigmund Abeles, Connecticut State Department of Education; Mrs. Grace Harrison, Director, Home Economics Division, Connecticut State Department of Education; and Ms. Constance Dimock. A special round of love and thanks go to my most enthusiastic pumpkin eaters, Geoffrey and Cassandra Purdy.

Contents

Before You Begin

If the arrangement of these recipes looks different to you, it is. In most recipes, ingredients are listed first, then you are told what to do with them. I have told you what foods to get ready in case you are going shopping, then listed ingredients and instructions when and where you actually use them. My testers find this method always works; I hope you will agree. I also hope you will have the patience to read all the way through a recipe before starting it. This will help you plan your time as well as your activities.

If you plan to use the metric measurements in this book, be sure to read the introductory chapter on measurements (see Contents). If you use the standard measurements, proceed as you ordinarily would.

With the help of this book, I hope you will discover the fun of creative cooking, as well as the pride of accomplishment when you make something others enjoy.

1. Safety: Keep pot handles turned away from the stove front so pots will not be bumped into and spilled. Turn off oven or stove-top as soon as you are through using it. When pots are removed from stove, place them on a heat-proof surface. To prevent fires, keep potholders, dishtowels, aprons, and your clothes away from stove burners. Keep a fire extinguisher in the kitchen just in case (and learn how to use it).

To prevent accidental cuts, store and wash knives separately from other utensils.

2. Butter: All butter used for the recipes in this book is lightly salted unless otherwise noted, when the recipe will say "sweet" butter. Margarine can almost always be substituted for butter, and in most recipes both are listed. In recipes that taste much better made with butter, margarine has been left off the ingredients list.

3. Flour: For better nutrition, use *unbleached* all-purpose flour instead of bleached. You will find the word *unbleached* on the front of the flour package. Flour is not sifted unless the recipe specifically calls for it. To sift flour, see index.

4. Sugar: Sugar is not sifted unless the recipe specifically calls for it. Turbinado (unrefined) sugar can be substituted for an equal amount of granulated white sugar. To substitute honey for granulated sugar, use about ⅞ as much (1 cup sugar = 250 ml = ⅞ cup honey = 220 ml) *and* use about 3 tablespoons (45 ml) *less* liquid in recipe.

5. Wheat germ: To increase nutritional value of recipes, we have added wheat germ wherever possible. We generally prefer to use unflavored toasted wheat germ, but raw unflavored wheat germ may be substituted.

6. Other health-food substitutions: To increase nutritional value of recipes, you can substitute 1 tablespoon (15 ml) sifted soy flour *plus* 1 tablespoon (15 ml) powdered dry milk *plus* 1 tablespoon (15 ml) wheat germ for an equal amount of flour in all cookie and cake recipes. NOTE: Soy flour causes quicker browning, so if you use it, lower oven temperature about 25°.

7. The timer: Whenever a recipe gives two times (such as 10 to 12 minutes), set your timer for the first time (10). Test for doneness. If necessary, reset timer for additional time (2 minutes) and cook longer.

8. Oven heat: Oven temperatures vary. It is very rare for the actual temperature inside the oven to be exactly the same as the one you set on the thermostat dial. If your foods do not cook in the time or manner described in the recipe, it may be because your oven is too hot, or not as hot as the heat indicated by your thermostat. To be safe, use a separate oven thermometer (sold in a hardware store) that hangs or sits on the oven shelf. Change the temperature on your outside thermostat dial until the inside oven temperature is correct. Please read the note about Celsius (metric) oven thermometers in the General Equipment List, see Contents.

9. Cleanliness: Whenever you are cooking, it is a good idea to wash your hands first and put on an apron. When you will actually be handling the ingredients in a recipe (as in shaping dough), a special hand-washing note is added to the recipe.

10. Cleanup: To keep other members of your family happy about your kitchen adventures, clean up when you are finished. To make this almost painless, fill up the sink with warm soapy water when you start to cook. Add dirty pots or spoons as they accumulate. Then they are soaked and ready to be washed (or to go into the dishwasher) when you are through cooking. Put ingredients away as soon as you are finished with them. Mop up spills as soon as they occur.

Measurements

This book is designed to be used EITHER with standard measurements OR with metric measurements. In each recipe, you will see both units listed side by side—for example, 1 cup flour (250 ml; 165 g). Select one method and use it consistently. If you choose to cook with the standard method, use the recipes as you ordinarily would, with standard measuring cups and spoons, and ignore the numbers in the parentheses. If you choose the metric system, don't convert, just cook! All the measurements you need are in the parentheses beside each ingredient; ignore the standard cup and spoon measurements. Use metric utensils or the widely available ones with markings in both standard and metric units. Before beginning to use metric measurements, be sure to read the metric information that follows.

All the measurements in this book are level. Thus, a cup (*or* 250 ml) of flour means that the cup is filled and then the top is leveled off with the blade of a knife (see Basic Skills—Contents).

STANDARD MEASUREMENTS

1 pinch	= less than ⅛ teaspoon
	= the amount you can pick up between your thumb and forefinger
1 level tablespoon	= 3 level teaspoons
¼ cup	= 4 tablespoons
⅓ cup	= 5⅓ tablespoons
½ cup	= 8 tablespoons
¾ cup	= 12 tablespoons
1 cup	= 16 tablespoons
	= 8 ounces (oz.)
2 cups	= 1 pint
2 pints	= 1 quart
4 quarts	= 1 gallon
8 ounces	= ½ pound
16 ounces	= 1 pound

METRIC MEASUREMENTS

Introduction

In cooking, we use three basic metric units: the *liter* (l), which measures volume (one l equals roughly 1 quart); the *gram* (g), which measures weight (1 g is roughly the weight of a paperclip), and the *meter* (m), which measures length (1 m equals roughly 1 yard). We also use other forms of these same units: the *milliliter* (ml), $1/1000$th of a liter (1 ml equals roughly ¼ teaspoon); the *kilogram* (kg), 1000 grams (1 kg equals a little over 2 pounds); and the *centimeter* (cm), $1/100$th of a meter (1 cm equals roughly ⅜″). Oven temperatures are measured in degrees Celsius (° C); 1° C is very roughly equal to 2° Fahrenheit. Here are some commonly used metric equivalents:

1 teaspoon	=	5 ml
1 tablespoon	=	15 ml
¼ cup	=	60 ml
⅓ cup	=	80 ml
½ cup	=	125 ml
¾ cup	=	185 ml
1 cup	=	250 ml

Oven temperature equivalents are:

Degrees Celsius (° C) roughly	= Degrees Fahrenheit (° F)
120–135	250–275
150–165	300–325
175–190	350–375
205–220	400–425
230–245	450–475

Metric Measuring Techniques

As a general rule, measuring techniques are the same in both the standard and the metric systems. That is, ingredients measured in standard cups you would measure in milliliter-marked cups; ingredients weighed on a scale in pounds you weigh on a metric scale in grams or kilograms.

We find the scale somewhat awkward to use and prefer whenever possible to use the simpler milliliter-marked utensils for most ingredients. You will find the ml units given where appropriate throughout the book. However, if you prefer to weigh your flour, sugar, and butter, for example, you will find their gram weights are also listed, alongside the ml, or volume, equivalents. (When the recipe says "measure," it also means "weigh.") We measure spices, extracts, and any very small (teaspoon or tablespoon) quantities of other ingredients only in milliliters, just as we do all liquids, oil, yogurt, honey, and so on. We list the weight of butter or margarine in grams only when more than ¼ cup; smaller quantities are measured in milliliters (1 tablespoon = 15 ml).

Using the Metric Scale

You will find that measuring weights in grams and kilograms can be a particularly variable thing. One day a cup (250 ml) of sugar will weigh 200 g, another time 210 g. The weights of flour and granulated and brown sugar, for example, vary depending upon the dampness of the weather, the brand of ingredient, and the scale itself. Spring-type scales are most commonly available and excellent to use for cooking, but are slightly less accurate than the beam-type scales, which are maddeningly precise and vary with the addition or subtraction of such tiny units as a single raisin. The point is, don't let our given gram weights intimidate you. They are approximate—your figures can vary as much as 20 grams up or down from ours and these recipes will still work. Remember, cooking is an art, not a science.

SPRING-TYPE SCALE

BEAM-TYPE SCALE

About Rounding Off Metric Measurements

Commercial measuring cups with both standard and milliliter markings have been rounded off to the nearest useful whole units. Thus, 1 cup is usually marked 250 ml. You should be aware that this is an approximation, which in most cases is close enough. But you may notice cases where there are discrepancies. For example, 1 cup butter = 16 tablespoons; 1 tablespoon = 15 ml; 16 tablespoons × 15 ml = 240 ml (not 250 ml). Don't try to figure out such apparent irregularities, just use the measurements as they are in this book. All our recipes have been tested with the metric quantities listed, and they work. We have also rounded off our metric quantities to their nearest useful whole units whenever possible (24.5 ml becomes 25 ml); ⅓ cup packed dark brown sugar = 85 g, but 1 cup is simplified to = 250 g instead of the actual 255 g.

Practical Examples

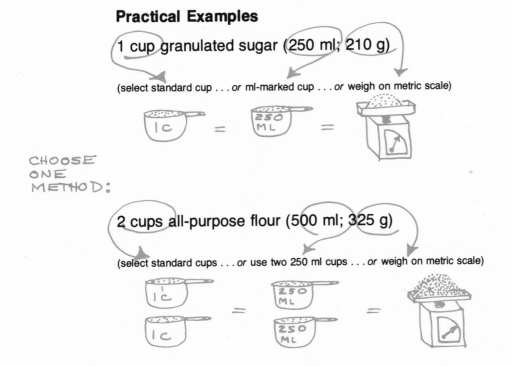

1 cup granulated sugar (250 ml; 210 g)

(select standard cup . . . *or* ml-marked cup . . . *or* weigh on metric scale)

CHOOSE ONE METHOD:

2 cups all-purpose flour (500 ml; 325 g)

(select standard cups . . . *or* use two 250 ml cups . . . *or* weigh on metric scale)

Basic Skills

To Level Measurements:

All measurements in this book are level unless otherwise specified. To level a measuring cup or spoon, fill it until slightly mounded, then draw the back of a knife blade over the top, scraping the surface flat.

To Measure Butter or Shortening:

Butter or margarine is easiest to measure when purchased in quarter-pound sticks.

1 pound	= 4 sticks	= 2 cups	= 480 ml	= 480 g
1 stick	= ½ cup	= 8 tablespoons	= 120 ml	= 120 g

Instead of measuring by the stick, you can pack the butter down very firmly into a measuring cup (be sure there are no air spaces trapped in the bottom), or you can use the "water displacement" method: To measure ¼ cup (60 ml) butter, fill a 1-cup (250 ml) measuring cup ¾ full (185 ml) with cold water. Add pieces of butter until the water reaches the 1-cup (250 ml) mark. Pour off water and you are left with ¼ cup (60 ml) measured butter.

To Sift Flour:

Sifting lightens the texture of baked goods. You can use either a strainer or a sifter for this process. Flour is sifted only where the recipe specifically calls for it.

Sift the required amount of flour onto a sheet of wax paper. Then pick up the paper, pull the edges around into a sort of funnel, and *gently* pour as much flour as you need back into a measuring cup. You can also use a spoon to transfer flour. Do not shake or pack measured flour. Level top of cup with knife blade, then add flour to recipe. Or return re-measured flour to sifter, add other dry ingredients, such as baking powder and salt, and sift everything together into the other ingredients in recipe.

To Weigh Sifted Flour:

Sift flour onto a piece of wax paper as explained above. Then spoon sifted flour lightly onto your wax-paper-lined scale until the measure is correct.

To Weigh Unsifted Flour:

Line the tray of your scale with a piece of wax paper. Spoon unsifted flour onto the wax paper until the measure is correct. Then gather up the paper and pour the measured flour from it into a sifter balanced on a mixing bowl, or spoon the flour into a sifter held over the bowl. Sift flour onto the other ingredients in recipe.

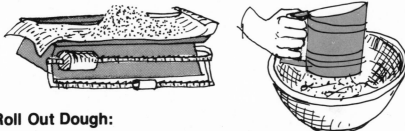

To Roll Out Dough:

There are two ways to roll out dough. One is on a countertop or a pastry board, the other between sheets of wax paper. If you are using a countertop or a pastry board, spread it lightly with flour so the dough will not stick. Also flour the rolling pin. Then roll out the dough, adding more flour if dough sticks. Some pastry boards and rolling pins are covered with cotton cloth (called a sock) to help prevent sticking; cloths should also be floured.

The second method is to cut two pieces of wax paper, each roughly 14″ (36 cm) long. Place one piece flat on the counter and flour it lightly. Place dough on floured paper, then sprinkle a little flour on top of dough. Cover dough with second paper. Use rolling pin (unfloured) to roll out dough between the papers. Peel the paper off and put it back on again if it gets too wrinkled. When dough is correct thickness, peel top paper off dough.

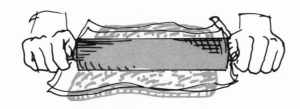

To Add Eggs to Recipe:

You may notice that whenever an egg is to be added to a bowl full of ingredients, it is first broken into a cup. That is so you can pick out the shells—should any accidentally fall in—before the egg disappears under the waves of flour or sugar in the bowl. I avoid asking you to add any "whole eggs" because I did that once in a cooking class and guess what happened? Right! Shell and all—just as requested.

To Separate an Egg:

Here are two different ways to separate an egg. The first method may be new to you, but try it anyway. It is very easy, never breaks the yolk, and is a lot of fun.

First wash your hands, as you will be touching the egg. Crack egg in half by tapping it sharply against side of bowl. Hold egg on its side as shown, grasping ends with your fingers. Fit tips of thumbs into crack. Pull shells apart and *at the same time* turn one half shell upright so it contains all the egg. Hold this shell, containing egg, upright with one hand while the other hand discards the empty half shell. Then turn empty hand palm up, fingers together, over a clean dry bowl. Pour out the entire egg onto the fingers of the empty hand. Spread fingers apart very slightly to let the egg white drip between them into the bowl while the yolk rests on top of the fingers as shown. Collect all of the white in a bowl; put yolk in a separate bowl.

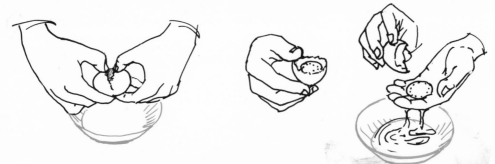

The most common procedure is to break egg in half, then hold half shell containing the yolk upright in one hand while you pour the egg white from the other half shell into a bowl. Then tip yolk out into the empty shell while white that surrounded it falls into bowl below. Place yolk in separate bowl.

To Use a Garlic Press:

A whole garlic bulb is made up of a cluster of separate cloves, each wrapped in its own thin skin. The easiest way to peel the skin off a clove of garlic is to set the clove on a wooden board or counter and smack it hard with the bottom of the garlic press. This breaks the skin so you can pick it off easily with your fingers.

To press the garlic, open the jaws of the garlic press. Set peeled clove inside, then press handles together, forcing garlic out through the holes into the bowl below. Use a spoon or knife to scrape off any pieces of garlic that cling on the outside of the holes. Discard the dry fibers left inside the press. NOTE: If you don't have a press, carefully chop the peeled garlic finely with a sharp knife.

To Chop an Onion:

"Chopping" with this method means you actually cut the onion into dice, or small pieces. First peel the onion. Then cut the onion in half lengthwise, from root to stem (a). Place one half, cut side down, on board. Hold it with fingers gripping sides, root end to the left (if you are right-handed). Slice onion as shown (b), with point of knife facing root end. Cut almost, but not all the way, through root end; this will help hold onion together. Finally, make narrow cuts in the opposite direction (c), cutting across the first slices to produce the "chopped" or diced pieces. Keep moving your fingers back away from the knife.

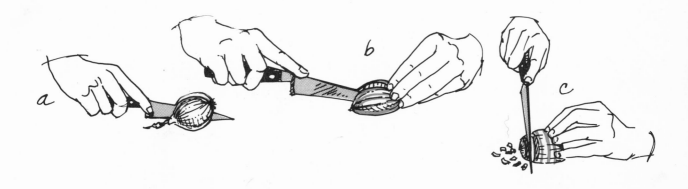

General Equipment List

Here is a list of all the equipment used in the preparation of the recipes. Each recipe will require the use of only a few items. This list is included as a guide; if you do not have the exact utensil specified, substitute whatever you think will work.

We have measured pots and pans to their *outside* edges, then noted how much water they hold when filled right to the very top. A round pan is measured across its center (the diameter). To see if your own pot is the same size, or nearly so, fill it up with carefully measured cups of water. Consider all metric measurements as approximate; use the utensils that come closest to ours in size.

Teacups *or* custard cups
Metric scale—optional; spring or balance-beam type (found in hardware *or* gourmet equipment shops)
Measuring cups and spoons, marked in standard and/*or* metric units (available in same places as metric scale)
Wooden spoon
Slotted *or* large *or* mixing spoon
Ice-cream scoop—optional
Ladle
Table knife, fork, teaspoon, butter knife (dull blade)
Long-handled fork
Tongs
Paring knife
Kitchen knife
Scissors, kitchen shears
Rubber scraper
Spatula
Pancake turner
Eggbeater
Wire whisk
Electric mixer
Colander

Sifter *or* strainer
Rolling pin
Pastry board—optional
Pastry blender—optional
Cookie cutters (*or* drinking glass turned upside down)
Wire rack
Cake tester *or* bamboo skewer
Toothpicks
Potato ricer *or* masher
Vegetable brush
Vegetable peeler
Grater
Garlic press
Blender—optional
Lemon squeezer *or* juicer
Lollipop sticks, Popsicle sticks (*or* new paint stirrers *or* thin wooden dowels found in hobby, craft, or dime stores)
Timer
Airtight container (such as plastic freezer box with lid *or* metal tin with lid)
Serving platter *or* tray
Wax paper, plastic wrap, aluminum foil

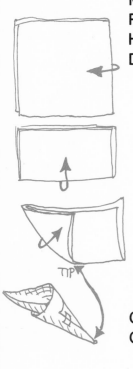

Paper *or* plastic bag

Muffin tin liners of paper *or* foil

Potholders

Heat-proof pad *or* trivet

Decorating tube (You can make your own by cutting a piece of wax paper about 12″ × 18″ (31 × 46 cm). Bring the short ends together to fold it in half, then in half again. Roll paper into a cone, with the tip along the folded edge as shown. Tape cone to hold it and cut off tip to make small hole. Fill with frosting, fold ends over, and squeeze down until frosting is forced out hole in tip)

Candy thermometer—optional

Oven thermometer—optional (See "Before You Begin," step 8. NOTE: Thermometers are available marked in standard and/*or* Celsius [metric] units. If you cannot locate a Celsius thermometer, you can calculate ° C approximately by dividing ° F in half. A moderate oven, 350° F = 175° C. A temperature conversion table is located in the introduction to "Metric Measurements": see index)

Double boiler

Ring mold *or* tube pan—9″ (23 cm) diameter, holds 6 cups (1.5 liters) water

Soup bowl—holds about 2 cups (500 ml) water

Mixing bowls: small—holds about 4 cups (1 liter) water; medium—8 to 10 cups (2 to 2.5 liters); large—14 to 16 cups (3.5 to 4 liters): this wide-topped bowl is used for mixing batter and dough

Oven-proof baking dish—1½ quart-size, about 8″ diameter, 2½″ deep (1.5 liters, 20 × 6 cm)

Saucepans with lids: small—holds about 4 cups (1 liter) water; medium—8 cups (2 liters) water; large—11 to 12 cups (2.75 to 3 liters)

Large pot *or* Dutch oven—holds 20 to 24 cups (5 to 6 liters) water

Electric skillet—optional

Frying pans: small—about 6″ (15 cm) diameter; medium—8″ to 9″ (20 to 23 cm) diameter; large—10″ to 12″ (25 to 31 cm) diameter

Roasting pan, medium-sized—about 13½″ × 9½″ × 2½″ (34 × 24 × 6 cm), holds 16 cups (4 liters) water

Bread pans (Dimensions of these pans will vary widely; as long as your pan is *approximately* the size specified, the recipe will be successful): large loaf—9¼″ × 5¼″ × 2¾″ (23.5 × 13 × 7 cm), holds 8 cups (2 liters) water; average loaf—9″ × 5″ × 3″ (23 × 13 × 8 cm), holds 8 cups (2 liters) water; medium loaf—8″ × 4¼″ × 2¼″ (20 × 11 × 6 cm), holds 4 cups (1 liter) water; baby loaf—6″ × 3½ ″ × 2″ (15 × 9 × 5 cm), holds 2 cups (500 ml) water

Cookie sheets (Flat, or with narrow edge. Cookies are easier to remove from an edgeless sheet. Shiny sheets bake and brown most evenly. Cookie sheet should not cover the entire oven shelf or it will block circulation of heat. For best results, use a sheet that allows at least 1½″ (4 cm) shelf space around all edges. To bake, place sheet on middle shelf of oven): small —13½″ × 10″ (34 × 25 cm); large—17 ″ × 14″ (43 × 36 cm)

Jelly roll pan—15½″ × 10½″ × 1″ (39.5 × 27 × 2.5 cm)

Muffin tin—2½″ cup size (6.5 cm)

Halloween Decorations
to Make and Eat

COOKIE PLACE CARDS:
LOLLIPOPS AND WITCHES' BROOMS

Use our quick and easy-to-make Scotch Shortbread recipe (see index) to make these place card cookies for your Halloween party table. Write each guest's name on a cookie with Decorative Frosting recipe that follows. For an extra-special touch, stand up each lollipop cookie in a bright red apple.

EQUIPMENT:
Same as for Scotch Shortbread (see index), *plus*:
Rolling pin
Wax paper *or* pastry board
Cookie cutters *or* paring knife
Spatula
Wire rack
Decorating tube (see General Equipment List)
Lollipop sticks *or* toothpicks (*or* bamboo saté skewers with pointed tips cut off)
Garlic press (to make broom straw)

FOODS YOU WILL NEED:
Same as for Scotch Shortbread, *plus*:
Decorative Frosting—recipe follows
Apples—1 whole red apple as a base for each lollipop place card

LOLLIPOP COOKIES

How To:

(One Scotch Shortbread recipe makes about
42 round cookies 2″ [5 cm] in diameter when
dough is rolled a scant ¼″ [0.5 cm] thick.)

1. Follow steps 1 to 3 of Scotch Shortbread recipe (see index). In step 3, add the tablespoon *or* 2 of milk so your dough is soft enough to roll out.

2. On a lightly floured pastry board *or* between 2 sheets of wax paper, roll dough (see Basic Skills) a fat ¼″ (0.5 cm) thick, *or* whatever thickness is necessary to hold the lollipop stick. Some sticks need dough ½″ (1 cm) thick.

3. Cut shapes in the rolled dough with cookie cutters *or* draw them freehand with the tip of a paring knife. Flour your spatula, then lift cookies and set them on *ungreased* cookie sheet. Poke the stick *or* toothpick *or* wooden skewer about halfway up inside each cookie.

4. Place cookie sheet in 325° F (165° C) oven and set timer to bake 10 to 12 minutes, or until cookies are golden around edges. Use potholders to remove pan from oven. Cool cookies on wire rack. Decorate with frosting (recipe follows), writing guests' names across the cookies. When frosting is hard to the touch, you can stick each lollipop into a shiny apple and set it on your party table.

WITCHES' BROOMS

How To:

(One Scotch Shortbread recipe makes about 22 Witches' Brooms)

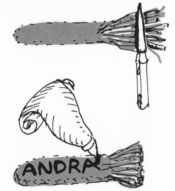

1. Follow directions for Lollipops, except shape cookies as follows:

   For each broomstick, roll a snake of dough about ½" (1 cm) thick and 3" *or* 4" (7 *or* 10 cm) long.

2. Put about 1 teaspoon of dough through a garlic press and cut the dough strings from the press with the tip of a knife.

3. Press your finger down on one end of each broomstick to make a flat spot. Dab a drop of water on this spot, then press on a section of the stringy dough to make the broom "straw." With knife, cut straight across the end of the straw.

4. Bake and decorate as for Lollipops, but write guest's name in frosting along broom handle. Set a broom at each guest's place at your party table.

DECORATIVE FROSTING

EQUIPMENT:
Small saucepan
Mixing bowl
Rubber scraper
Measuring cups and spoons
Sifter
Large spoon, teaspoon
Custard cups *or* teacups—1 for each color
   you will tint frosting
Decorating tube(s)—(see General Equipment List)

FOODS YOU WILL NEED
2 tablespoons butter *or* margarine (30 ml)
2 cups confectioners' sugar (500 ml; 250 g)
1 teaspoon vanilla extract *or* strained lemon juice (5 ml)
2 *or* 3 tablespoons milk *or* cream (30-45 ml)
Vegetable food coloring *or* canned beet juice (for red color) and concentrated frozen orange juice (for yellow and orange color), Baker's cocoa (for brown)

Ingredients:

(To make about ¾ cup, 185 ml)

2 tablespoons butter *or* margarine (15 ml)
2 cups confectioners' sugar (500 ml; 250 g)
1 teaspoon vanilla extract *or* strained lemon juice (5 ml)
2 *or* 3 tablespoons milk *or* cream

3. Frosting should be of a consistency that will spread easily. If it feels too stiff, add more milk *or* cream, 1 teaspoon (15 ml) at a time. If it feels too soft, sift in a little more sugar.

How To:

1. Place butter *or* margarine in small saucepan and set over low heat until melted. Remove from heat and set aside.

2. Sift sugar into bowl. Add melted butter, cleaning pan with rubber scraper. Add vanilla *or* lemon juice and milk *or* cream. Beat until smooth.

4. Place a couple of tablespoons of frosting in each cup. Blend in a few drops of coloring; to make orange color, mix a few drops of beet juice with a tablespoon or 2 of frozen orange juice. Add more sifted sugar if frosting softens after coloring. In another cup sift in a tablespoon of Baker's cocoa for chocolate brown color. Put frosting into decorating tube and squeeze out fancy designs.

CARAMEL CANDIED APPLE GOBLINS

Glaze your apples with caramel, then trim them with nuts or candies to create a gallery of goblins for Halloween party favors.

EQUIPMENT:
Wax paper
Small tray
Wooden sticks—new paint stirrers *or* Popsicle sticks *or* short wooden dowels found in craft *or* hobby shops
Measuring cups and spoons
Large saucepan with lid
Wooden spoon
Teaspoon
Timer
Candy thermometer—optional; *or* drinking glass

FOODS YOU WILL NEED:
2½ tablespoons butter *or* margarine (40 ml)
4 to 6 medium-sized apples
1½ cups packed light brown sugar (375 ml; 155 g)
6 tablespoons water (90 ml)
Glass of water *plus* 2 ice cubes—optional
Trimming: halved nuts *or* assorted candies, including licorice shoestring candy, *or* breakfast cereals, seedless raisins, shredded coconut, etc.

Ingredients:

(To make 4 to 6 medium-sized candied apples)

1 tablespoon butter *or* margarine (15 ml)

4 to 6 medium-sized apples

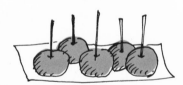

1½ cups packed light brown sugar (375 ml; 155 g)
6 tablespoons water (90 ml)
1½ tablespoons butter *or* margarine (25 ml)

How To:

1. Cut a sheet of wax paper large enough to hold the apples and grease it with butter or margarine. Set greased paper on tray.

2. Wash and dry apples. Remove stems, poke a stick into the stem end of each apple, and set them on tray.

3. Measure sugar and water into saucepan. Mix with wooden spoon to dissolve sugar, then add butter *or* margarine.

4. Set saucepan on stove over medium heat and bring sugar to a boil. Cover pan with lid for 3 minutes, so steam can wash the sugar crystals down pan sides. Then uncover pan and *turn off heat.*

5. If you have a candy thermometer, *carefully* clip it onto the side of the pan. It should be on a slant so the tip does not rest directly on pan bottom. If you do not have a thermometer, set a glass of ice water beside stove.

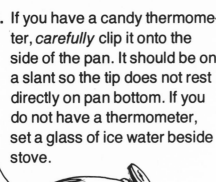

6. Turn on medium heat under pan and boil syrup. When lots of bubbles rise up, lower heat slightly, so syrup bubbles slowly. Boil 4 or 5 minutes, *or* until thermometer reads about 260° F (130° C), "hard-ball stage," *or* until a drop of syrup turns into a hard ball when spooned into a glass of ice water. Pinch ball between your fingers to test. If too soft, cook syrup a few *seconds* longer and retest; don't overcook, or syrup will taste burned. Turn off heat when done.

7. Remove pan from stove, and set on heat-proof surface beside prepared tray of apples. Hold apples by their sticks and dip them, one at a time, into syrup. Tip pan a little as you do this, so apples are completely coated with syrup. Then set apples, sticks up, on greased wax paper. Syrup will stay soft in pan 5 or 6 minutes; hardened syrup can be softened by setting pan on stove over *very* low heat and stirring with wooden spoon.

8. Caramel glaze hardens on apples in about 10 minutes. While apple's glaze is still soft, stick on bits and pieces of nuts, candies, *or* cereal to make faces, hair, beards, and so on. If you need more "glue" as glaze hardens, dab the candies with soft warm (*not* hot) syrup from bottom of pan before attaching them to apples. In warm *or* damp weather, store candied apples in the refrigerator. To wash utensils, soak them in hot water until syrup dissolves.

PEANUT BUTTER BUGS

Add a few simple ingredients to your favorite type of peanut butter and create this versatile modeling clay that doubles as a nutritious snack. With it you can make all sorts of creepy-crawly things to decorate your Halloween party table.

EQUIPMENT:
Mixing bowl
Large spoon
Measuring cups and spoons
Paring knife *or* kitchen shears
Wax paper *or* plastic wrap

FOODS YOU WILL NEED:
¼ cup peanut butter (60 ml; 75 g)
1 tablespoon wheat germ (15 ml)
1 tablespoon honey (15 ml)
2½ tablespoons nonfat dry milk, instant *or* noninstant type (40 ml)
Licorice shoestring candy

Ingredients:

How To:

(To make ½ cup mixture [125 ml] , for about 12 bugs)

¼ cup peanut butter, chunky or smooth type (60 ml; 75 g)

1 tablespoon wheat germ (15 ml)

1 tablespoon honey (15 ml)

2½ tablespoons nonfat dry milk, instant *or* noninstant type (40 ml)

Licorice shoestring candy

TURTLE

WING LOOPS

CROSS LICORICE LEGS

THEN ADD PEANUT BUTTER BODY

1. In mixing bowl, combine peanut butter, wheat germ, honey, and dry milk. Mix with spoon. Add a little more dry milk, if necessary, to make mixture dry enough to model like clay.

2. Wash your hands. Form peanut-butter mixture into 12 balls, each about 1″ (2.5 cm) in diameter. Model each ball into any shape you like: snakes, bugs, snails, centipedes, and so on, and set on wax paper *or* plastic wrap.

3. With knife *or* shears, cut short pieces of licorice shoestring candy and poke them into your bugs to make legs, eyes, antennae, and so forth. Bend long pieces around into loops to make wings. Eat immediately, or chill in refrigerator until ready to serve.

BLACK CATS

Dip marshmallows in melted chocolate, then stack and trim them with candies to make appealing and edible favors for your Halloween party table.

EQUIPMENT:
Measuring cups
Double boiler *or* large and small frying pans
Kitchen shears—optional
Paring knife
Wax paper
Flat plate *or* small tray (a size that will fit in refrigerator *or* freezer)
Tongs *or* long-handled fork
Wooden spoon
Rubber scraper
Toothpicks

FOODS YOU WILL NEED:
Water
Large (12-ounce, 350 g) package semisweet chocolate bits (enough to cover 8 to 10 cats)
32 regular-size marshmallows
Licorice shoestring candy
24 pieces of corn candy (triangular-shaped orange candies sometimes called "hen's teeth")
16 silver dragée candies *or* cinnamon hots (*or* other small round candies)

Ingredients:

How To:

(To make 8 cats)

Water
12-ounce package semisweet chocolate bits (500 ml; 350 g)

32 whole marshmallows

1. Place about 1″ (2.5 cm) water in bottom of double boiler *or* ½″ (1 cm) water in large frying pan, and set pan on stove over medium heat. Measure chocolate into top of double boiler *or* small frying pan and set it over the simmering (slowly boiling) water until chocolate is melted—about 5 minutes.

2. While chocolate is melting, prepare the various parts of the cats. Use kitchen shears *or* paring knife to cut 16 whole marshmallows into quarters (*or* smaller bits) to make 4 little feet for each cat. (NOTE: You can leave feet off altogether if you prefer.) Set feet aside on a piece of wax paper placed on a flat plate *or* tray. Alongside feet, place 16 whole marshmallows.

Licorice shoestring candy
24 whole pieces of triangle-
 shaped corn candy
16 silver dragée candies *or*
 cinnamon hots

TURN TIP
UPSIDE DOWN
FOR NOSE

3. On another piece of wax paper nearby, set out the following: 8 licorice shoestring tails, each cut about 3″ (8 cm) long, and 32 shoestring licorice whiskers, each about 1″ (2.5 cm) long. Cut 8 pieces of corn candy in half crosswise and save the triangle-shaped tips to make 8 noses. Set out 16 whole corn candies for ears and 16 silver dragées *or* cinnamon hots for eyes.

4. Remove pan of melted chocolate from stove and set it on heat-proof surface. Set marshmallows nearby.

5. With tongs *or* long-handled fork, dip all the whole marshmallows and marshmallow pieces into chocolate. Push pieces around until well coated, then set pieces on wax-paper-covered plate *or* tray.

6. Working while chocolate is soft (it stays this way at least 30 minutes, so you don't have to rush), complete the head sections of the 8 cats. To do this, stick candy pieces for ears, noses, eyes, and whiskers directly into the warm chocolate on 8 whole coated marshmallows, as shown. Set them on

covered tray *or* plate. NOTE: If candy pieces droop or slide down, don't worry; they can be reset later with a little more warm chocolate.

7. To make hind sections, poke one licorice tail into the rear of each remaining whole marsh-mallow. Stick 4 chocolate-coated feet into the soft choco-late around the bottom edge of each hind section. With head and hind sections sitting sepa-rately on wax paper, place plate *or* tray in refrigerator for about 30 minutes (*or* in freezer for 15 minutes) until chocolate is very hard.

8. To complete cats, remove the sections from the refrigerator and lift each piece up off the wax paper.

   Use a toothpick as shown to connect head and hind sec-tions of each cat. Now that chocolate is hard, it will not melt if stored in a cool, dry place. In hot weather, store in refrigerator. Cats can be made ahead of your party and stored upright in a box *or* plastic bag in the refrigerator *or* freezer. If frozen, defrost before serving. Remove toothpicks before eating.

POKE TAIL IN

PUSH DOWN

TOOTHPICK

PUSH UP

SEÑOR SQUASH CENTERPIECE

Create this humorous figure with any vegetables you happen to have around. The head can be any sort of squash, or a pumpkin, or even a big, lumpy potato. Radishes, carrots, celery, and other edibles make the features, which are either poked into holes or held in place with toothpicks. Let Señor Squash be your Halloween party centerpiece as well as your salad.

EQUIPMENT:
Pencil and paper—optional
Small paring knife
Toothpicks (preferably strong round wooden or plastic type)
Aluminum foil—optional
Flat plate or tray

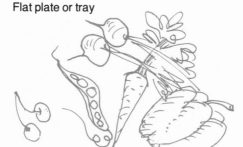

FOODS YOU WILL NEED:
to make one centerpiece
(use the following or any substitutions you prefer)
Whole fresh squash or pumpkin or potato—any size
2 whole red radishes
1 whole carrot
2 stalks of celery
8 to 10 whole cherry tomatoes—optional
1 whole red or green bell pepper
1 bunch of parsley or watercress
Red or green cabbage or lettuce
Apple—optional

How To:

(To make 1 centerpiece)

1. Wash all vegetables carefully to remove any dirt.

2. Take a good look at your basic head shape—the squash or pumpkin or potato—and decide what personality it has and what type of face you can create with it. You may want to make a few sketches with pencil and paper before you begin with the vegetables. Let your imagination be your guide. You can make full standing figures or any type of animal in the same way. You can copy our design or make up your own.

CUT

CROWN

3. For the hat *or* crown, cut a red *or* green bell pepper as shown. First remove the top and bottom, then cut the narrower end into points, keeping the ring whole. Set hat or crown in place around stem of squash (top of head) and fasten in place with toothpicks set at an angle between the pepper's bottom edge and the top of the head.

4. Use the tip of the paring knife to make holes in the head just large enough to poke in the whole radishes (stem ends inward) for the eyes and a whole carrot (point out) for the nose. Make arm holes on each side just large enough to contain a stalk of celery. For the mouth, you can attach a whole cherry tomato with a toothpick, or cut a mouth-shaped piece of leftover red *or* green pepper and attach it with a toothpick. Make a parsley *or* watercress mustache held on with toothpicks. Do hair the same way, or make it from strips of red cabbage leaves, cut into a fringe. Fringed cabbage leaves can be cut for eyelashes, *or* you can use celery leaves held on with toothpicks.

MOUTH

EYELASHES

ARMS:
CELERY
OR
ASPARAGUS

5. Make a bow tie with the remaining scraps of pepper, *or* use a slice of apple. *Or* make a whole ring of aluminum foil *or* cherry tomatoes around the base of the head to form a sort of collar. Set the finished figure on a plate *or* tray on a bed of cabbage *or* lettuce leaves. Be sure to remove toothpicks before eating vegetables.

Brunch and Lunch

FRIED PUMPKIN BLOSSOMS

This unusual recipe is an Italian specialty known as *Fritto di Fiori di Zucca.* If you have a garden with lots of pumpkin or squash blossoms, you will find this recipe fun to try. But don't pick all the flowers—leave some to ripen into jack-o'-lanterns. Serve your fried blossoms with a green salad and Whole Wheat Pumpkin or Zucchini Bread (see index) for lunch.

EQUIPMENT:
Mixing bowl
Wire whisk *or* fork
Measuring spoons and cups
Metric scale—optional
Paper *or* plastic bag—lunch-bag size
Wax paper—optional
Plate—optional
Large frying pan
Tongs
Paper towels

FOODS YOU WILL NEED:
About 12 fresh pumpkin (*or* squash) blossoms (4 to 6 per serving)
1 egg
½ cup all-purpose flour (125 ml; 80 g)
¼ teaspoon salt (1.2 ml)
¼ teaspoon pepper (1.2 ml)
2 teaspoons grated Parmesan cheese (10 ml)
Vegetable oil

Ingredients:

(To make about 12 blossoms, to serve 2 to 3 people)

About 12 fresh pumpkin *or* squash blossoms

1 egg

½ cup all-purpose flour (125 ml; 80 g)
¼ teaspoon salt (1.2 ml)
¼ teaspoon pepper (1.2 ml)
2 teaspoons grated Parmesan cheese (10 ml)

Vegetable oil

How To:

1. Pick blossoms. Pick off stems and remove threads from center of each flower. Wash flowers under running water.

2. Beat egg in mixing bowl with whisk *or* fork. Measure flour, salt, pepper, and cheese into bag.

3. Dip each blossom into egg, then drop it into bag and shake gently to coat with flour mixture. Set coated blossoms on wax paper.

4. Put about ½" (1 cm) of oil in bottom of frying pan and set on stove over medium heat. Use tongs to gently set down coated blossoms in hot oil. Turn when golden on bottom (1 *or* 2 minutes). Brown on other side, drain on paper towels. Serve hot, with a sprinkle of salt.

HARD-BOILED MICE

Trim half a hard-boiled egg to create the tastiest mouse that ever crept across a Halloween party plate.

EQUIPMENT:
Saucepan
Timer
Potholder
Small sharp paring knife
Wax paper
Vegetable peeler—optional
Serving plate

FOODS YOU WILL NEED:
Eggs—½ egg for each serving
1 raw carrot
Whole cloves—2 for each mouse
Celery stalks *or* licorice shoestring candy—1 piece for each mouse
Lettuce leaves—1 piece for each mouse

Ingredients:

(Plan on ½ egg for each serving)

Eggs—at room temperature (*or* warmed a few minutes in a bowl of warm water)

How To:

1. First, hard-boil as many eggs as you will need. To do this, gently place whole eggs in saucepan. Add cold water until it reaches about 1″ (2.5 cm) above top of eggs. Set pan over medium heat and bring water to boil. Lower heat slightly and boil gently for 15 minutes for medium to large eggs *or* 12 minutes for small eggs.

2. When done, turn off stove. Hold handle of pan with potholder and *carefully* carry pan to the sink. Run cold water into the pan until eggs feel cool enough to touch. Remove eggs from water and set them aside to cool 20 to 30 minutes. *Or* refrigerate them overnight if you want to do this step ahead of time.

1 raw carrot

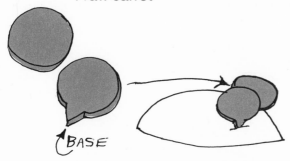

BASE

for each mouse you will need:
2 whole cloves
1 celery stalk *or* length of
  licorice shoestring candy
1 piece of lettuce leaf

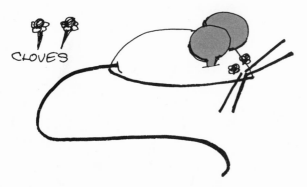

CLOVES

3. When ready to trim cold eggs, tap and roll their shells gently on table. Peel them. (Peel warm eggs under cold running water if you don't have time to cool them.)

4. Slice eggs in half lengthwise and set them cut side down on wax paper.

5. Wash and peel carrot. To make ears for each mouse, cut 2 carrot slices, each about the size and thickness of a nickel. Cut a pointed base in each slice, as shown, then stick points into egg just above *narrow* end.

6. To make eyes, stick 2 cloves into each egg, as shown. (Don't eat whole cloves.) For whiskers, cut 4 short lengths of licorice shoestring candy *or* 2 toothpick-size sticks of celery. Poke them into front end of each mouse. For tail, cut 1 longer piece of licorice *or* celery and poke it into back end of mouse. Set each mouse on a piece of lettuce on a plate and serve.

CRUNCHY GRANOLA CEREAL

Granola cereal is made from different combinations of whole natural grains, chopped dried fruits, seeds, and nuts. You can vary the recipe depending upon which ingredients you have around. Forget that granola is full of vitamins and very good for you and think about how crunchy and delicious it is to eat, whether in a bowl with milk for breakfast or baked into Peanut Butter–Granola Cookies (see index).

EQUIPMENT:
Metric scale—optional
Measuring cups and spoons
Large mixing bowl
Large spoon—optional
Jelly roll *or* roasting pan (with sides about 1″ [2.5 cm] *or* higher)
Timer
Potholders
Clean, empty jars with lids

FOODS YOU WILL NEED:
2 cups old-fashioned rolled oats (500 ml; 180 g)
1 cup rye flakes (250 ml; 100 g), *or* soy *or* bran flakes
½ cup wheat germ (125 ml; 60 g)
¼ cup sesame seeds (60 ml; 40 g)
½ cup sunflower seeds (125 ml; 80 g)
¼ cup shredded coconut (60 ml; 40 g)
½ cup chopped walnuts (125 ml; 65 g), *or* chopped almonds
1 teaspoon salt (5 ml)
½ cup honey (125 ml)
½ cup vegetable oil—such as peanut *or* safflower (125 ml)
1 cup seedless raisins (250 ml; 160 g), *or* chopped dates *or* chopped dried apricots

Ingredients:

(To make 6 to 7 cups, about 1½ pounds or slightly over 0.5 kg)

2 cups old-fashioned rolled oats (500 ml; 180 g)

1 cup rye flakes (250 ml; 100 g), *or* soy *or* bran flakes

½ cup wheat germ (125 ml; 60 g)

¼ cup sesame seeds (60 ml; 40 g), hulled *or* unhulled

½ cup sunflower seeds (125 ml; 80 g)

¼ cup shredded coconut (60 ml; 40 g)

½ cup chopped walnuts (125 ml; 65 g), *or* chopped almonds

1 teaspoon salt (5 ml)

½ cup honey (125 ml)

½ cup vegetable oil—such as peanut *or* safflower (125 ml)

1 cup seedless raisins (250 ml; 160 g), *or* chopped dates *or* chopped dried apricots

How To:

1. Turn oven on to 250° F (120° C).

2. Wash your hands. Measure grains, seeds, coconut, nuts, and salt into mixing bowl. Blend all ingredients together with your hands.

3. Drip honey and oil over cereal in bowl. Mix with hands *or* spoon until cereal is evenly coated.

4. Spread cereal out over pan and flatten it down with palm of your hand. Place pan in 250° F (120° C) oven and set timer to toast cereal for 60 minutes. When done, remove pan from oven with potholders. Let cereal cool until comfortable to touch.

5. Crumble up cereal and mix in dried raisins *or* other dried fruit. Store cereal in airtight jars.

WHOLE WHEAT PUMPKIN BREAD AND MUFFINS

Serve warm pumpkin muffins for breakfast on Halloween morning or slices of pumpkin bread with cider or hot cocoa after trick-or-treating. This quick and easy-to-make recipe is extra good made with whole wheat flour, but unbleached white flour can be successfully substituted. NOTE: For a less sweet recipe, use all the honey, but only ¼ cup (60 ml; 55 g) granulated sugar.

EQUIPMENT:

Measuring cups and spoons
Large mixing bowl
Metric scale—optional
Mixing spoon *or* wire whisk *or* electric
    mixer
Rubber scraper
Muffin tin—2½"-cup size (6.5 cm); *or* bread
    loaf pan—about 9" × 5" × 3" (23 × 12.5
    × 7.5 cm)
Timer
Toothpick
Potholders
Wire rack

FOODS YOU WILL NEED:

2 tablespoons butter *or* margarine (30 ml)
2 eggs
¾ cup granulated sugar (185 ml; 165 g)
¾ cup honey (185 ml)
½ cup vegetable oil (125 ml)
1 cup canned *or* fresh pumpkin, cooked
    and mashed (250 ml; 240 g)—to cook
    fresh pumpkin, follow directions for
    Jack-o'-Lantern Beef Stew (see index)
¼ cup water (60 ml)
1¾ cups whole wheat flour (435 ml; 225 g)
    or all-purpose flour (435 ml; 285 g)
2 tablespoons wheat germ (30 ml)
1 teaspoon baking powder (5 ml)
½ teaspoon baking soda (2.5 ml)
1 teaspoon salt (5 ml)
½ teaspoon ground nutmeg (2.5 ml)
½ teaspoon cinnamon (2.5 ml)
½ teaspoon ground allspice (2.5 ml)
¼ teaspoon ground cloves (1.2 ml)

Ingredients:

How To:

(To make 12 muffins or 1 loaf)

1 *or* 2 tablespoons butter *or* margarine (15 *or* 30 ml)

2 eggs
¾ cup granulated sugar (185 ml; 165 g)
¾ cup honey (185 ml)
½ cup vegetable oil (125 ml)
1 cup canned *or* fresh pumpkin, cooked and mashed (250 ml; 240 g)—to cook fresh pumpkin, see index
¼ cup water (60 ml)
1¾ cups whole wheat flour (435 ml; 225 g) *or* all-purpose flour (435 ml; 285 g)
2 tablespoons wheat germ (30 ml)
1 teaspoon baking powder (5 ml)
½ teaspoon baking soda (2.5 ml)
1 teaspoon salt (5 ml)
½ teaspoon ground nutmeg (2.5 ml)
½ teaspoon cinnamon (2.5 ml)
½ teaspoon ground allspice (2.5 ml)
¼ teaspoon ground cloves (1.2 ml)

1. Turn oven on to 350° F (175° C). Grease pan with butter *or* margarine.

2. Break eggs into mixing bowl. Mix all other ingredients together with eggs in bowl. Beat until well blended.

3. Spoon batter into pan. Muffin cups should be about ⅔ full. Clean bowl sides with rubber scraper.

4. Place pan in 350° F (175° C) oven and bake loaf for 60 minutes *or* muffins for 45 to 55 minutes. They are done when top is golden and a toothpick stuck into center of batter comes out clean. Remove pan from oven with potholders and cool thoroughly. Remove bread from pan and set on wire rack.

ZUCCHINI BREAD

This delicately flavored bread is seasoned with Parmesan cheese and smells as delicious as it tastes. It is quick and easy to make. Toast it, or serve buttered slices with Witches' Caldron Cider Soup (see index) for lunch.

EQUIPMENT:

Loaf pan—9″ × 5″ × 3″ (23 × 12.5 × 7.5 cm)
Metric scale—optional
Grater
Wax paper
Paring knife
Cutting board
Measuring cups and spoons
Small saucepan
Rubber scraper
Large mixing bowl
Mixing spoon *or* wire whisk
Timer
Toothpick *or* cake tester
Potholders
Wire rack

FOODS YOU WILL NEED:

6½ tablespoons butter *or* margarine (100 ml; 100 g)
½-pound piece of raw zucchini squash (about 200 g)
½ medium-sized onion
2 eggs
1 cup buttermilk (250 ml) *or* 1 cup minus 2 tablespoons whole milk (220 ml) *plus* 2 tablespoons vinegar (30 ml)
3 cups all-purpose flour (750 ml; 500 g)
2 tablespoons wheat germ (30 ml)
2 tablespoons granulated sugar (30 ml)
3 tablespoons grated Parmesan cheese (45 ml)
5 teaspoons baking powder (25 ml)
½ teaspoon baking soda (2.5 ml)
1½ teaspoons salt (7.5 ml)

Ingredients:

(To make one loaf)

½ to 1 tablespoon butter *or* margarine (7.5 to 15 ml)

½-pound piece of raw zucchini squash (about 200 g)

How To:

1. Turn oven on to 350° F (175° C). Grease pan with butter *or* margarine, *or* substitute vegetable oil.

2. Wash zucchini but do *not* peel it. Grate it over a piece of wax paper, using the side of the grater with the largest holes. Measure 1 cup (250 ml) of grated zucchini, packing it down firmly into cup. Drain off any excess liquid. Then empty cup onto another piece of wax paper, and set it aside.

½ medium-sized onion

5½ tablespoons butter *or* margarine (85 ml; 85 g)

2 eggs
1 cup buttermilk (250 ml) *or* 1 cup minus 2 tablespoons whole milk (220 ml) *plus* 2 tablespoons vinegar (30 ml)

3 cups all-purpose flour (750 ml; 500 g)
2 tablespoons wheat germ (30 ml)
2 tablespoons granulated sugar (30 ml)
3 tablespoons grated Parmesan cheese (45 ml)
5 teaspoons baking powder (25 ml)
½ teaspoon baking soda (2.5 ml)
1½ teaspoons salt (7.5 ml)

3. Peel onion half, then chop it finely (see Basic Skills). You should have about 2 tablespoons (30 ml). Set onion aside on another piece of wax paper.

4. Measure butter *or* margarine into small saucepan and set it on stove over low heat until melted. Remove from stove. Use rubber scraper to empty butter into large mixing bowl.

5. Add eggs to measuring cup one at a time, then add them to melted butter in bowl. Add buttermilk (*or* regular milk *plus* vinegar) and the chopped onion that was set aside. Beat with whisk *or* spoon to blend well.

6. Stir grated zucchini into egg-milk-onion mixture in bowl. Add flour, wheat germ, sugar, cheese, baking powder, baking soda, and salt. Stir slowly until well blended.

7. Spoon batter into greased pan. Clean sides of bowl with rubber scraper. Place pan in 350° F (175° C) oven and set timer to bake for 55 to 60 minutes, *or* until toothpick *or* cake tester inserted in center of bread comes out clean. Remove pan from oven with potholders. Cool bread about 20 minutes, then tip it out of pan and set on wire rack.

GREEN PEPPER MONSTERS

Can you eat your green monster before he eats you? Since he's really a salad, you will win if you're very brave . . . and hungry. At a luncheon party, your guests might enjoy making their own monsters if you set out all the pieces.

EQUIPMENT:
Paring knife
Teaspoon
Vegetable peeler
Toothpicks

FOODS YOU WILL NEED:
(For 1 monster):
1 whole raw green (or sweet red) bell pepper
½ cup of your favorite egg or tuna-fish salad (125 ml)
1 small raw carrot
2 whole cloves
3 or 4 flower clusters of raw broccoli or cauliflower or celery leaves
1 lettuce leaf

Ingredients:

How To:

(To make 1 monster)

1 whole raw green (*or* sweet red) bell pepper

½ cup of your favorite egg *or* tuna-fish salad (125 ml)

1 small raw carrot
2 whole cloves

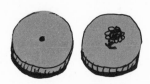

1. Wash pepper. Cut around stem end and lift it out. Use teaspoon or fingers to pull seeds and white membrane out of pepper. Rinse inside with water to remove loose seeds.

2. At end opposite stem, cut out a mouth with jagged teeth. Use pepper's lumpy shape for nose, chin, and so on, as shown. Fill pepper (from stem end) with any salad you like.

3. To make eyes, peel carrot. Then cut 2 slices, each about ¼" (0.5 cm) thick. Poke a hole in the center of each slice with toothpick, then stick a clove in each hole to make pupil of eye.

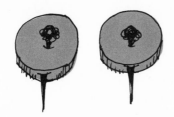

4. Break a toothpick in half. Stick broken end of each half into the edge of a carrot slice (like a lollipop). Then attach eyes by sticking sharp toothpick ends into top of monster's head, as shown.

TOOTHPICK

5. To make end of nose, cut pointy tip off carrot (*or* carve cone shape from a small carrot section). Stick one end of a toothpick into flat end of shape, then poke other end of toothpick onto tip of monster's pepper nose.

ARMS

TOOTH PICK   HAIR

6. To make arms, cut 2 carrot sticks, about ¼″ (0.5 cm) on each side and 3″ (7 cm) long. Use point of paring knife to make 1 small arm hole on each side of monster. Poke a carrot stick into each hole.

3 or 4 flower clusters of raw broccoli *or* cauliflower *or* celery leaves
1 lettuce leaf

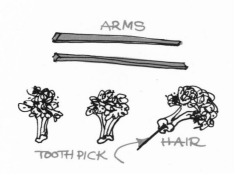

7. For hair, break off 3 or 4 small flowers of broccoli *or* cauliflower, *or* use celery leaves. Use toothpicks, as shown, to connect pieces. To do this, poke a toothpick into stem of each flowerlet *or* leaf, then poke other end of toothpick into top of monster's head. Set each monster on a lettuce leaf and serve. *Or* make monsters ahead of time and refrigerate until needed.

WITCHES' CALDRON CIDER SOUP

Any witch or warlock could be proud to serve this steaming soup from a pumpkin caldron. Be sure to add the salty, crisp croutons to complement the soup's mellow apple-cider flavor.

EQUIPMENT:

Metric scale—optional
Paring knife
Large spoon and wooden spoon
Flat serving platter
Measuring cups and spoons
Small frying pan
Fork
Small serving bowl *or* soup bowl
Large saucepan
Large mixing bowl
Eggbeater *or* wire whisk
Ladle

FOODS YOU WILL NEED:

1 whole pumpkin—about 6 pounds (3 kg)
　or larger

3 tablespoons butter *or* margarine (45 ml)
1 slice bread, any type
¼ teaspoon salt (1.2 ml)
3 cups apple cider (750 ml)
2 tablespoons packed dark brown sugar
　(30 ml)
1½ tablespoons cornstarch (25 ml)
¾ cup cold milk (185 ml)
2 eggs
1 tablespoon granulated sugar (15 ml)
⅛ teaspoon ground ginger (0.5 ml)
½ teaspoon cinnamon (2.5 ml)
½ teaspoon ground nutmeg (2.5 ml)
Dash of ground cloves

Ingredients:

(To make 4 to 5 servings; about 4 cups [1 liter] of soup. NOTE: To make more, double the recipe but *use just 3 eggs)*

1 whole pumpkin—about 6 pounds (3 kg) *or* larger

3 tablespoons butter *or* margarine (45 ml)
1 slice bread (use more if you wish)
¼ teaspoon salt (1.2 ml)

How To:

1. Wash outside of pumpkin to remove any dirt. Cut out the lid of the pumpkin as you would for a jack-o'-lantern *but* make the cuts at least 2½" (6 cm) away from the stem so the opening will be big enough to ladle out the soup. Scoop out all seeds and membranes with spoon. Save seeds to roast (see index). Place pumpkin on serving platter and set it aside.

2. To make croutons, melt butter *or* margarine in small frying pan over low heat. Set bread in melted butter. When bread is browned and toasted on the bottom, turn it with fork and

(46)

3 cups apple cider (750 ml)
2 tablespoons packed dark
    brown sugar (30 ml)

1½ tablespoons cornstarch
    (25 ml)
¼ cup cold milk (60 ml)

2 eggs
½ cup cold milk (125 ml)
1 tablespoon granulated sugar
    (15 ml)
⅛ teaspoon ground ginger
    (0.5 ml)
½ teaspoon cinnamon (2.5 ml)
½ teaspoon ground nutmeg
    (2.5 ml)
Dash of ground cloves

brown on other side. Sprinkle both sides of toast with salt. Remove pan from stove. Cut toast into very small pieces, about ½″ (1 cm) square, and place them in small serving bowl on table.

3. Measure cider into large saucepan. Add brown sugar, stir, and set aside.

4. In large mixing bowl, combine cornstarch and milk and stir with spoon until smooth.

5. In same bowl, add eggs, the rest of the milk, sugar, and spices. Beat with eggbeater *or* whisk until well blended.

6. Place saucepan of cider on stove over medium-high heat. Bring cider to a full bubbling boil, then turn off heat. Set pan on heat-proof surface beside bowl of egg-milk mixture.

7. Ladle about 1 cup (250 ml) of hot cider out of pan and pour it directly into bowl of egg-milk mixture to warm it up. Immediately beat with whisk *or* eggbeater.

8. As soon as you have warmed the egg-milk mixture, ladle or pour *all* of it directly back into the pan of hot cider. Stir *or* whisk the mixture. Don't worry if liquid looks curdled—it will smooth out when cooked.

9. Return saucepan to stove and set it over low heat. Whisk *or* stir constantly with wooden spoon about 4 *or* 5 minutes. Soup should thicken until it looks like heavy cream and coats a spoon that is dipped in it. Mixture should be smooth and no longer look curdled. Remove pan from stove and *carefully* pour *or* ladle hot soup into prepared pumpkin on platter. Serve soup while hot, ladling out each serving, then sprinkling it with a few croutons from the small bowl.

Various Vegetables

PUMPKIN PUDDING

This sweet and spicy dish is more like a soufflé than a pudding. It is very easy to make and can be served as a vegetable, with roast meat or hamburgers and hot dogs, or as a warm dessert with a spoon of vanilla yogurt or ice cream. You can substitute baked sweet potatoes or acorn squash for the pumpkin. NOTE: This is a good way to use up any pumpkin left over from Jack-o'-Lantern Beef Stew (see index).

EQUIPMENT:
1½-quart baking dish, about 8″ diameter and 2½″ deep (1.5 liter size, about 20 cm diameter and 6 cm deep)
Medium-sized mixing bowl
Wire whisk *or* wooden spoon
Electric mixer *or* eggbeater
Measuring cups and spoons
Potato ricer *or* masher
Rubber scraper
Timer
Potholders

FOODS YOU WILL NEED:
2 eggs
4 tablespoons butter *or* margarine (60 ml), at room temperature
⅓ cup honey (80 ml)
¼ cup milk (60 ml)
½ teaspoon salt (2.5 ml)
¼ teaspoon ground nutmeg (1.2 ml)
⅛ teaspoon cinnamon (0.5 ml)
⅛ teaspoon ground ginger (0.5 ml)
2 tablespoons wheat germ (30 ml)
1 cup canned *or* fresh pumpkin, cooked and mashed (250 ml; 240 g)—to cook fresh pumpkin, follow Jack-o'-Lantern Beef Stew recipe (see index)

Ingredients:

(To make 4 or 5 servings, ½ cup [125 ml] each)

2 eggs

ONLY YOLKS

4 tablespoons butter *or* margarine (60 ml), at room temperature
⅓ cup honey (80 ml)

How To:

1. Turn oven on to 350° F (175° C). Separate eggs (see Basic Skills), and put yolks into baking dish. Put whites into mixing bowl and set aside.

2. Add butter and honey to egg yolks in baking dish and beat well with whisk *or* wooden spoon.

¼ cup milk (60 ml)

½ teaspoon salt (2.5 ml)

¼ teaspoon ground nutmeg (1.2 ml)

⅛ teaspoon cinnamon (0.5 ml)

⅛ teaspoon ground ginger (0.5 ml)

2 tablespoons wheat germ (30 ml)

1 cup canned *or* fresh pumpkin, cooked and mashed (250 ml; 240 g)—to cook fresh pumpkin, see index

3. Add milk, salt, spices, wheat germ, and pumpkin to egg-yolk mixture in baking dish and beat well.

4. Use electric mixer *or* egg-beater to beat egg whites in mixing bowl until they form stiff peaks.

5. Use rubber scraper to spoon egg whites into pumpkin mixture. Fold in whites gently by turning the rubber scraper upside down as you pull it slowly through the pumpkin mixture. Don't stir hard; you want to keep the air in the whites so they will make the pumpkin light.

6. Clean off the top edges of the baking dish with the rubber scraper, pushing the mixture *gently* down toward the bottom of dish. Place baking dish in 350° F (175° C) oven. Set timer to bake for 40 minutes. Remove from oven with potholders and set on heat-proof surface. Serve warm directly from baking dish.

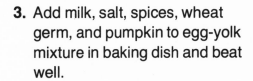

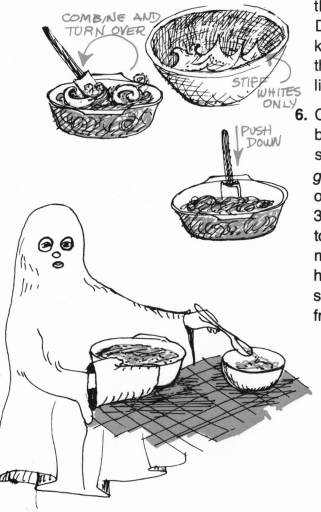

COMBINE AND TURN OVER

STIFF WHITES ONLY

PUSH DOWN

INDONESIAN CORN FRITTERS

Try these crisp fritters for an unusual and easy way to serve corn. They are cooked like pancakes in a frying pan or electric skillet and do not require an oven. They may be made right in a classroom if you like. To give these *Frikadel Djagung* an authentic Indonesian flavor, add the coriander and scallions.

The fritters are delicious for lunch served with a green salad and sausages or cold meat. For dinner, serve them with Country-style Spare Ribs or Orange Chicken (see index). Leftover fritters are rare, but if you find any, you'll discover they are even good cold.

EQUIPMENT:
Strainer—optional
2 mixing bowls
Measuring cups and spoons
Eggbeater *or* wire whisk
Paring knife—optional
Large spoon
10″ or 12″ frying pan (25 to 30 cm) *or* electric skillet
Pancake turner
Potholders
Oven-proof platter—optional
Heat-proof pad *or* trivet

FOODS YOU WILL NEED:
2 cups corn kernels—frozen, canned, *or* fresh (500 ml; about 300 g)
2 eggs
2½ tablespoons all-purpose flour (40 ml)
½ teaspoon salt (2.5 ml)
⅛ teaspoon pepper (0.5 ml)
¼ teaspoon ground nutmeg (1.2 ml)
½ teaspoon ground coriander (2.5 ml)—optional
1 scallion—optional
1 tablespoon butter *or* margarine *or* vegetable oil (15 ml)

Ingredients:

(To make about 10 fritters, 3″ [7.5 cm] in diameter)
2 cups corn kernels (500 ml; about 300 g)—canned, frozen, *or* raw and freshly sliced from cob *by an adult*

How To:

1. Drain canned corn through a strainer. Defrost frozen corn before using. To do this quickly, set corn in a bowl over a pan of hot water and stir occasionally; drain in strainer before using. Measure prepared corn into a mixing bowl.

2 eggs
2½ tablespoons all-purpose
  flour (40 ml)
½ teaspoon salt (2.5 ml)
⅛ teaspoon pepper (0.5 ml)
¼ teaspoon ground nutmeg
  (1.2 ml)
½ teaspoon ground coriander
  (2.5 ml)—optional
1 scallion (optional)

1 tablespoon butter *or* margarine *or* oil (15 ml)

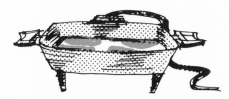

2. Break eggs into second mixing bowl. Add flour and seasonings. Beat well with eggbeater *or* whisk. Add corn and stir well.

3. If you wish to add a scallion, wash it under running water. Cut roots off white bulb end. With knife, slice it into thin ¼″ (0.5 cm) sections. Add to egg-corn batter and stir.

4. Add butter *or* margarine *or* oil to frying pan *or* electric skillet. Place pan over medium heat *or* turn electric skillet on to 350° F (175° C).

5. When butter sizzles in pan *or* skillet, place 3 *or* 4 heaping tablespoonfuls (45 *or* 60 ml) of batter slightly apart from each other in the pan, just as if you were making pancakes. Turn down heat if butter burns *or* oil smokes. Cook fritters 3 *or* 4 minutes, *or* until bubbles appear in them and their tops lose their shine and seem firm around the edges. Use pancake turner to turn fritters over. Cook them 2 *or* 3 minutes longer, until bottoms are lightly browned.

6. Remove fritters from pan and serve them immediately, while repeating step 5 to make more. You shouldn't need to add more butter to pan. You can eat the first batch while the second is cooking. *Or* you can keep fritters warm on an oven-proof platter in a 200° F (100° C) oven, adding more until all are cooked. Remove platter from the oven with potholders and serve fritters hot.

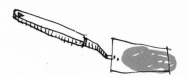

BAKED ACORN SQUASH

If you have ever tried to cut a raw acorn squash in half, you know how hard that job can be. Try our simplified method in which the squash is baked whole, then sliced and seasoned. Serve baked squash in place of potatoes with any roast meat, a green vegetable, and a salad. You can use squash baked this way in any recipe calling for pumpkin or sweet potatoes.

EQUIPMENT:
Vegetable brush
Metric scale—optional
Shallow oven-proof baking dish
Timer
Potholders
Knife
Large spoon
Measuring spoons

FOODS YOU WILL NEED:
2 whole acorn squash (½ squash for each serving); each about 2½ pounds (1 kg)
4 tablespoons butter *or* margarine (60 ml)
4 tablespoons honey *or* brown sugar *or* maple syrup (60 ml)
Dash of cinnamon *and* ground nutmeg

Ingredients:

(To serve 4; plan on ½ squash for each serving)

2 whole 2½-pound acorn squash (1 kg each)

How To:

1. Turn oven on to 350° F (175° C). Wash squash with vegetable brush and water. Place whole squash on baking dish and set in oven. Set timer to bake for 60 minutes.

2. Remove baked squash from oven with potholders. Leave heat on. Cool squash until comfortable to touch—about 10 minutes—then cut each squash in half crosswise, as shown.

In *each* squash half add:
  1 tablespoon butter *or* margarine (15 ml)
  1 tablespoon honey *or* brown sugar *or* maple syrup (15 ml)
  Dash of cinnamon *and* ground nutmeg

3. Use spoon to scoop out seeds and membranes and discard them.

4. Set halves, cut sides up, in baking dish. If they lean over too much, prop them upright against each other, *or* lean them against an overturned oven-proof custard cup. Measure butter, honey, and spices into each squash half.

5. Return pan to oven. Set timer to bake for 30 minutes, so seasoning cooks into squash. Remove pan from oven with potholders. Serve each half squash upright in a small bowl.

Main-Dish Meats

JACK-O'-LANTERN BEEF STEW

Put stew in a pumpkin shell and there you'll serve it very well! Especially for a Halloween dinner party, with Zucchini Bread (see index) and a green salad. Adapted from *Carbonada Criolla,* a regional specialty of Argentina, this South American dish involves several steps and is a good project for several cooks to work on together. The stew and pumpkin are prepared separately, then baked and served together.

EQUIPMENT:
Metric scale—optional
Vegetable brush
Paring knife, kitchen knife
Large spoon
Shallow oven-proof baking dish large enough to hold your pumpkin
Timer
Potholders
Table fork
Cutting board
Dutch oven with lid
Garlic press
Aluminum foil *or* soup bowl
Wooden spoon
Vegetable peeler
Measuring cups and spoons
Long-handled fork
Heat-proof pad *or* trivet
Black oil-base felt-tipped pen—optional

FOODS YOU WILL NEED:
1 whole pumpkin—6 pounds (3 kg) *or* larger
5 tablespoons margarine *or* butter (75 ml; 75 g)
¼ teaspoon cinnamon (1.2 ml)
¼ teaspoon ground nutmeg (1.2 ml)
2 medium-sized yellow *or* white onions
2 cloves of garlic
2 pounds stewing beef—chuck (1 kg), cut into bite-sized pieces
1 large carrot
2 medium-sized sweet *or* white potatoes
2 medium-sized whole tomatoes
8 dried apricot *or* peach halves
1½ cups frozen *or* fresh peas *or* corn kernels (375 ml; 225 g)
¼ cup seedless raisins (60 ml; 40 g)
½ teaspoon salt (2.5 ml)
¼ teaspoon pepper (1.2 ml)
¼ teaspoon dried thyme (1.2 ml)
¼ teaspoon cinnamon (1.2 ml)
2 cups beef bouillon *or* water (500 ml)

TO COOK PUMPKIN

Ingredients:

How To:

(To make 6 to 8 servings)

1 whole pumpkin—6 pounds (3 kg) or larger

2 tablespoons butter *or* margarine (30 ml)
¼ teaspoon cinnamon (1.2 ml)
¼ teaspoon ground nutmeg (1.2 ml)

NOTE: Follow steps 1 to 4 to cook any fresh pumpkin. Instead of using it for this stew, you can also peel and cube *or* mash it and serve it as you would squash *or* sweet potatoes.

1. Turn oven on to 350° F (175° C). Wash outside of pumpkin with vegetable brush and water to remove dirt. Cut out the lid of the pumpkin as you would for a jack-o'-lantern, *but* cut the lid about 2½″ to 3″ (6 to 8 cm) out from the stem. This opening must be large enough for you to reach inside holding the serving spoon.

2. With the lid off, scrape out seeds and membranes. Save seeds to toast (see index).

3. Place butter *or* margarine and the spices inside pumpkin. Cover with lid, and place pumpkin on oven-proof dish. Set it in 350° F (175° C) oven and set timer to bake for 60 minutes. During this time, prepare the stew as described in stew directions following.

4. After 60 minutes, use potholders to remove pumpkin (on its dish) *carefully* from oven. Set on heat-proof surface. To test doneness, lift lid, wait a few seconds for steam to subside, then stick a table fork into the pumpkin flesh near the opening. It should feel quite soft, like a baked potato. If done, set pumpkin aside on heat-proof surface and turn off oven. If still too hard, return it to oven and bake until soft. Pumpkin may be baked ahead of time and kept unrefrigerated up to 3 hours before filling and baking with stew.

TO MAKE STEW

Ingredients:	How To:
(To make 6 to 8 servings)	NOTE: Stew can be made the day before and refrigerated until needed.

2 medium-sized yellow *or* white onions

1. Chop onions (see Basic Skills) on cutting board.

3 tablespoons butter *or* margarine (45 ml)
2 cloves of garlic

2 pounds stewing beef—chuck (1 kg)

2. Add butter *or* margarine to Dutch oven and set it on stove over medium heat. Add chopped onions. Press both cloves of garlic (see Basic Skills) into pan with onions. Sauté (fry gently) onions and garlic until golden, stirring every now and then with wooden spoon. When done, spoon onion-garlic mixture out of pan and set it aside on foil *or* in soup bowl.

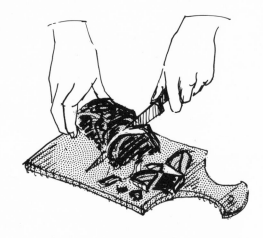

3. Cut beef into serving pieces, then add it to the same pan that onion was cooked in. Turn on heat to medium and brown beef on one side, then turn it with wooden spoon *or* long-handled fork. After meat is browned on both sides, turn off heat. Sprinkle cooked onion-garlic mixture over meat in pan.

1 large carrot

4. Peel carrot, then cut it up into roughly 2″ (5 cm) lengths and add them to beef.

2 medium-sized sweet *or* white potatoes
2 medium-sized tomatoes

5. Wash and peel potatoes. Cut them into approximately 1″ (2.5 cm) cubes. Add to beef. Wash and remove stems from tomatoes. Cut them into small pieces and add to beef.

8 dried apricot *or* peach halves
1½ cups frozen *or* fresh peas *or* corn kernels (375 ml; 225 g)
¼ cup seedless raisins (60 ml; 40 g)
½ teaspoon salt (2.5 ml)
¼ teaspoon pepper (1.2 ml)
¼ teaspoon dried thyme (1.2 ml)
¼ teaspoon cinnamon (1.2 ml)
2 cups beef bouillon *or* water (500 ml)

6. Add fruit, peas, raisins, and bouillon *or* water to meat mixture. Stir with wooden spoon. Cover pan with lid and set on stove over medium-low heat. When mixture boils, turn down heat and simmer (cook slowly over low heat) about 60 minutes, *or* until meat feels tender when stuck with a fork. When done, turn off heat, remove pan from stove and set it aside on heat-proof-surface until about 45 minutes before serving. (Refrigerate stew if waiting longer than a couple of hours.)

TO ASSEMBLE

1. 45 minutes before serving, preheat oven to 350° F (175° C). Spoon stew into baked pumpkin, which should be sitting on its baking dish. Any stew that does not fit can be left in the pan to be reheated later. Put the lid on the pumpkin and return it to the hot oven. Set timer to bake 30 minutes.

2. To test doneness, lift pumpkin's lid. Stew inside should be steaming hot.

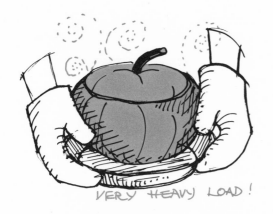

VERY HEAVY LOAD!

3. *Very carefully* use potholders to remove pan with pumpkin from the oven. Remember, the pumpkin is full and extra-heavy. You may need to ask an adult to help with this step. Set pan on heat-proof pad on table.

4. If you wish, you can use a felt-tipped pen to draw a jack-o'-lantern face on the side of the baked pumpkin. *Be careful not to pierce the pumpkin's skin with the pen.* Do not eat the skin with the drawing on it! To serve, scoop or ladle out some pumpkin along with the stew.

ORANGE CHICKEN

This slightly sweet and very tangy chicken is a relative of the French *Poulet à l'Orange.* The recipe is easy to prepare, and fun for several cooks to work on together. For a Halloween dinner, or a party at any time of the year, serve Orange Chicken with Indonesian Corn Fritters (see index) *or* rice and a salad.

EQUIPMENT:
Metric scale—optional
Wax paper
Large platter *or* tray
2 medium-sized mixing bowls
Wire whisk *or* eggbeater
1 clean paper *or* plastic bag, lunch-bag size
Measuring cups and spoons
Large frying pan, at least 12″ (30 cm) in diameter
Tongs *or* long-handled fork
Dutch oven *or* large pot with lid
Garlic press
Paring knife
Cutting board
Timer
Table fork

FOODS YOU WILL NEED:
1 frying chicken, about 3 pounds (1.5 kg), cut up into serving pieces
1 egg
⅓ cup all-purpose flour (80 ml; 55 g) *or* whole wheat flour
½ teaspoon salt (2.5 ml)
½ teaspoon pepper (2.5 ml)
¼ cup vegetable oil (60 ml)
1 clove of garlic
¼ cup raw green pepper, chopped (60 ml; 50 g)
1 teaspoon prepared regular mustard (5 ml)
2 tablespoons soy sauce (30 ml)
1 tablespoon unsulfured-type molasses *or* honey (15 ml)
3 tablespoons tomato sauce *or* catsup *or* prepared chili sauce (45 ml)
1 cup orange juice (250 ml)
1 whole orange

Ingredients:

(To serve 4)

1 frying chicken about 3 pounds (1.5 kg), cut up into serving pieces
1 egg

⅓ cup all-purpose flour (80 ml; 55 g) *or* whole wheat flour
½ teaspoon salt (2.5 ml)
½ teaspoon pepper (2.5 ml)

How To:

1. Place cut-up chicken parts on wax paper set on a platter. Break egg into one bowl and beat it up with whisk *or* egg-beater.

2. In paper *or* plastic bag, measure flour, salt, and pepper. Dip each piece of chicken in turn into egg in bowl, then drop it into bag of flour. Close top of

¼ cup vegetable oil (60 ml)

DUTCH OVEN

1 clove of garlic
¼ cup raw green pepper,
   chopped (60 ml; 50 g)
1 teaspoon prepared regular
   mustard (5 ml)
2 tablespoons soy sauce
   (30 ml)
1 tablespoon molasses *or*
   honey (15 ml)
3 tablespoons tomato sauce *or*
   catsup *or* chili sauce (45 ml)
1 cup orange juice (250 ml)

1 whole orange

bag and shake gently to coat chicken with flour. Set piece of chicken on wax paper and repeat with rest of chicken.

3. Measure oil into frying pan and set it on stove over medium heat. When oil is hot enough to quickly brown a drop of egg-flour batter you gently set into it, *gently* add chicken, 1 piece at a time, *with tongs. Don't drop chicken in, or oil will splatter you.*

4. Fry chicken until bottom side is golden brown, then turn with tongs *or* long-handled fork and brown on other side. This takes 7 to 10 minutes, approximately. Pick up each browned piece with tongs and set it into Dutch oven or pot. Turn off heat under frying pan.

5. While chicken is browning, you can start preparing sauce. Press garlic (see Basic Skills) into second bowl. Finely chop green pepper into approximately ¼″ (0.5 cm) bits, using paring knife on cutting board. Then measure and add pepper to bowl. Add mustard, soy sauce, molasses *or* honey, tomato sauce *or* catsup *or* chili sauce, and orange juice. Stir well.

6. Pour bowl of sauce over chicken in Dutch oven *or* pot. Cover with lid and set on stove over low heat. Set timer to simmer chicken in sauce about 30 minutes, *or* until a meaty piece of chicken feels tender when pricked with a fork.

7. While chicken is simmering, peel orange with paring knife. Then cut it crosswise into cartwheel slices a little less than ½″ (1.5 cm) thick. Pick out seeds. Set slices on wax paper. About 5 minutes before chicken is done, add sliced orange to pot, then replace lid. Serve chicken directly from pot with sauce and a slice of orange.

COUNTRY-STYLE SPARE RIBS

While regular spare ribs are bony, "country-style" ribs are very meaty because they are actually pork chops that the butcher cuts from a rib-end roast sliced in half. Serve them with rice *or* Indonesian Corn Fritters (see index). NOTE: This sauce is also good on regular spare ribs.

EQUIPMENT:
Metric scale—optional
Knife
Medium-sized roasting pan, about 13½" × 9½" × 2½" (34 × 24 × 6 cm)
Garlic press
2 small mixing bowls
Measuring cups and spoons
Mixing spoon
Timer
Potholders
Long-handled fork
Small dish

FOODS YOU WILL NEED:
2½ pounds country-style pork chops (1 kg)
1 clove of garlic
¼ teaspoon ground ginger (1.2 ml)
¼ teaspoon dried thyme (1.2 ml)
¼ teaspoon dried oregano (1.2 ml)
⅛ teaspoon salt (0.5 ml)
¼ teaspoon pepper (1.2 ml)
2 tablespoons soy sauce (30 ml)
1 tablespoon prepared mustard (15 ml)
2 tablespoons tomato sauce *or* catsup (30 ml)—optional
1 tablespoon honey *or* maple syrup (15 ml)
1 cup orange *or* cranberry *or* apple juice (250 ml)

Ingredients:

(To serve 3 or 4)

2½ pounds country-style spare ribs (1 kg)

How To:

1. Turn oven on to 350° F (175° C). Cut as much fat as possible off outside of meat. Place meat in roasting pan and set it aside.

1 clove of garlic

¼ teaspoon ground ginger (1.2 ml)

¼ teaspoon dried thyme (1.2 ml)

¼ teaspoon dried oregano (1.2 ml)

⅛ teaspoon salt (0.5 ml)

¼ teaspoon pepper (1.2 ml)

2 tablespoons soy sauce (30 ml)

1 tablespoon prepared mustard (15 ml)

2 tablespoons tomato sauce *or* catsup (30 ml)—optional

1 tablespoon honey *or* maple syrup (15 ml)

1 cup orange *or* cranberry *or* apple juice (250 ml)

2. Press garlic into mixing bowl (see Basic Skills). Add all other ingredients and stir with spoon. Pour sauce over meat. Turn each piece of meat over in sauce.

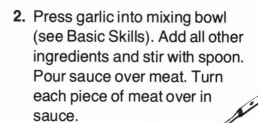

3. Place pan in 350° F (175° C) oven and set timer for 30 minutes. When time is up, remove pan from oven with potholders and turn ribs over with long-handled fork. If sauce is too dry, add about ½ cup (125 ml) more fruit juice or water. Whether or not you added more sauce, return pan to oven now and set timer for additional 15 minutes. Total cooking time is 45 minutes.

4. When time is up, remove pan from oven and set on a heat-proof surface. Cut into meat; it is done when no longer pink. If it needs more baking, return to oven and check again after about 15 minutes. When meat is done, use spoon to skim fat from pan into a small dish. Serve ribs hot with some pan juices. Cool fat, then discard.

Treats and Sweets

PURPLE POISON PUNCH

Halloween is full of surprises and this recipe is one of them—it tastes unexpectedly delicious!

EQUIPMENT:
Measuring cups and spoons
Punch bowl
Large spoon
Ladle
Serving cups

FOODS YOU WILL NEED:
4 cups cold milk (1 liter)
2 cups chilled ginger ale (500 ml)
1 cup cold unsweetened grape juice
   (250 ml)
1½ cups vanilla ice cream (375 ml)

Ingredients:

(To make 10 servings, approximately ⅔ cup each)

4 cups cold milk (1 liter)
2 cups chilled ginger ale
   (500 ml)
1 cup cold unsweetened grape
   juice (250 ml)

1½ cups vanilla ice cream (375
   ml; 260 g)

How To:

1. Combine all ingredients in punch bowl. Stir with ladle.

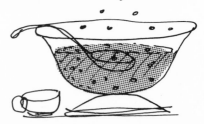

2. Use spoon to cut ice cream into small pieces. Serve punch with ladle, adding a piece of ice cream to each cup.

YUMMMM!

TOASTED PUMPKIN SEEDS

After you carve your jack-o'-lantern, save the seeds to make this tasty snack. Follow the procedure below whether you have a tiny pumpkin with a few seeds or a giant with several cups of seeds; add more salt for more seeds. Store cooled seeds in airtight can *or* jar.

EQUIPMENT:
Paring knife
Large spoon
Colander
Jelly roll pan *or* oven-proof frying pan
Measuring spoons
Timer
Potholders
Airtight can *or* jar

FOODS YOU WILL NEED:
Seeds from medium-sized *or* larger fresh pumpkin—3½-pound (1.5 kg) pumpkin gives you about ¾ cup (80 ml; 50 g) seeds
1 to 3 tablespoons salt (15 to 45 ml)

Ingredients:

Fresh pumpkin seeds—any amount

1 to 3 tablespoons salt (15 to 45 ml)—*or* more to taste

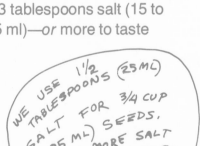

WE USE 1½ TABLESPOONS (25 ML) SALT FOR ¾ CUP (185 ML) SEEDS. USE MORE SALT IF YOU PREFER.

How To:

1. Turn oven on to 300° F (150° C).

2. Prepare pumpkin as you would for a jack-o'-lantern, cutting off the top and scooping out the seeds and membranes. Place seeds in a colander.

3. Wash seeds under warm water in colander. Spread damp seeds flat on jelly roll pan *or* oven-proof frying pan. Sprinkle seeds with as much salt as you like.

4. Place pan in 300° F (150° C) oven and set timer to bake for 20 to 30 minutes, *or* until seeds are dry and crisp. Remove pan from oven with potholders. Set on heat-proof surface until seeds are cold.

SHERBET JACK-O'-LANTERNS
IN CHOCOLATE SHELLS

You can make these fancy chocolate candy shells in just a few minutes, then fill them with a scoop of your favorite sherbet *or* ice cream *or* pudding. Orange sherbet and chocolate bits turn them into cheery Halloween jack-o'-lanterns. *Or* use cut-up bits of fresh strawberries, grapes, *or* other fruits to make dessert faces for any party.

EQUIPMENT:

Large and small frying pans *or* double
    boiler
Measuring cups and spoons
12 paper muffin-tin liners
Muffin tin
Teaspoon
Flat serving platter *or* tray
Ice-cream scoop *or* large spoon
Plastic wrap—optional

FOODS YOU WILL NEED:

Water
1¼ cups semisweet chocolate bits (310
    ml; 225 g)
1 tablespoon butter *or* margarine (15 ml)
6 scoops orange sherbet (1 pint; 500 g) *or*
    ice cream *or* pudding)

Ingredients:

(To make 6 filled chocolate shells)

Water
1 cup semisweet chocolate bits (250 ml; 175 g)
1 tablespoon butter *or* margarine (15 ml)

PAPER LINER

How To:

1. Place about ½" (1 cm) water in large frying pan *or* 1" (2.5 cm) in bottom of double boiler and set pan on stove over medium heat. Measure chocolate and butter *or* margarine into smaller pan *or* top of double boiler and set it over simmering water until chocolate is melted.

2. While chocolate is melting, set 2 paper liners in each of 6 muffin cups (the double paper is stronger for handling).

3. When chocolate is soft, remove it from stove. Stir well with spoon, then set it aside about 3 minutes to cool slightly, *but not harden.*

4. Working with 1 muffin cup at a time, spoon about 1½ tablespoons (25 ml) melted chocolate into the paper liner. Hold paper at the top edge while you spread the chocolate all over the inside surface, using the back of the spoon. Draw chocolate up from the bottom, forcing it into the paper folds on the sides. Coating will be quite thick. Repeat with all cups.

1 pint orange sherbet (500 g) *or* ice cream *or* pudding
¼ cup chocolate bits (60 ml; 50 g) *or* any other small candies *or* fresh fruits

5. Set muffin tin in refrigerator *or* freezer until chocolate is very hard (about 5 minutes in freezer, a little longer in refrigerator). When hardened, carefully lift chocolate cups out of muffin pan and set them on a table, platter, *or* tray to warm up slightly—about 3 to 5 minutes.

6. After this warm-up, paper should peel off chocolate without any difficulty. To do this, hold each cup carefully with your fingers on the inside and outside edges of the bottom (rather than squeezing in on the sides). Peel paper off, then set cups on platter *or* tray.

PEEL OFF PAPER

7. To make jack-o'-lanterns, fill each cup with a scoop of orange sherbet. Then arrange chocolate bits *or* other candies into a face on top. *Or,* instead of sherbet, use your favorite ice cream or pudding, trimmed with bits of fresh fruit. You can make these before your party and store them until needed on a platter in the freezer covered with plastic wrap.

APPLE-OAT BARS

A layer of apples and nuts is sandwiched between chewy oat cookies in this delicious snack or dessert. Try a bar topped with vanilla ice cream or yogurt.

EQUIPMENT:
Vegetable peeler
Paring knife
Cutting board
Wax paper
Measuring cups and spoons
Metric scale—optional
9″ (23 cm) square baking pan about 1½″ (4 cm) deep
Large mixing bowl
Large spoon
Grater—optional
Timer
Potholders
Sifter

FOODS YOU WILL NEED:
2 medium-sized apples
½ cup (1 stick) *plus* 1 tablespoon butter *or* margarine (135 ml; 135 g), at room temperature
⅔ cup packed dark brown sugar (160 ml; 170 g)
1 egg
1 teaspoon vanilla extract (5 ml)
1 cup all-purpose flour (250 ml; 165 g) *or* whole wheat flour (250 ml; 130 g)
½ teaspoon baking soda (2.5 ml)
½ teaspoon salt (2.5 ml)
½ teaspoon ground nutmeg (2.5 ml)
1 teaspoon cinnamon (5 ml)
⅛ teaspoon ground ginger (0.5 ml)
1 teaspoon grated orange rind (5 ml)—optional
2 tablespoons wheat germ (30 ml)
1⅓ cups old-fashioned rolled oats (330 ml; 120 g)
½ cup finely chopped walnuts (125 ml; 65 g)
¼ cup confectioners' sugar (60 ml; 30 g)

Ingredients:

How To:

(To make about 25 bars)

2 medium-sized apples

1. Wash and peel apples. Use paring knife to cut them into quarters on cutting board, then cut away core sections. Slice apples in approximately ¼″ (0.5 cm) thick slices and set them aside on wax paper.

1 tablespoon butter *or* margarine (15 ml)

½ cup (1 stick) butter *or* margarine (120 ml; 120 g), at room temperature

⅔ cup packed dark brown sugar (160 ml; 170 g)

1 egg

1 teaspoon vanilla extract (5 ml)

1 cup all-purpose flour (250 ml; 165 g) *or* whole wheat flour (250 ml; 130 g)

½ teaspoon baking soda (2.5 ml)

½ teaspoon salt (2.5 ml)

½ teaspoon ground nutmeg (2.5 ml)

1 teaspoon cinnamon (5 ml)

⅛ teaspoon ground ginger (0.5 ml)

1 teaspoon grated orange rind (5 ml)—optional

2 tablespoons wheat germ (30 ml)

1⅓ cups old-fashioned rolled oats (330 ml; 120 g)

½ cup finely chopped walnuts (125 ml; 65 g)

PAT DOWN DOUGH

APPLES   NUTS

2. Turn oven on to 350° F (175° C). Grease pan with butter *or* margarine.

3. Measure butter *or* margarine and brown sugar into bowl and mix them together with large spoon.

4. Add egg and vanilla to bowl and beat well.

5. Mix flour, baking soda, and salt into ingredients in bowl. Stir in spices.

6. Add grated orange rind if you have it, wheat germ, and rolled oats. Wash your hands, then use them, *or* large spoon, to blend all ingredients together well.

7. Dip your hands in flour, then pat *half* the dough into the bottom of the greased pan. Spread apple slices evenly over the dough. Sprinkle nuts over apples. Dip fingers in

NUTS + APPLES

PRESS ON MORE DOUGH

flour, then press remaining dough into a layer covering apple-nut mixture. Press top dough down flat with palm of your hand. Dough should cover apples completely.

PRESS

8. Place pan in 350° C (175° C) oven and set timer to bake for 30 minutes, or until slightly golden around edges. Use potholders to remove pan from oven and set on heat-proof surface. Let cool in pan until top is just comfortable to touch.

9. Cut a sheet of wax paper about the size of the baking pan. Set paper on top of dough in pan. With palm of your hand, push down firmly all over paper, to press the top dough layer onto the center apple layer. (Don't touch the hot pan.) If dough still feels too hot, place a potholder on the wax paper under your hand before pressing.

¼ cup confectioners' sugar
(60 ml; 30 g)

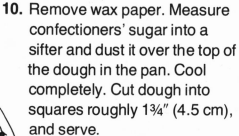

10. Remove wax paper. Measure confectioners' sugar into a sifter and dust it over the top of the dough in the pan. Cool completely. Cut dough into squares roughly 1¾" (4.5 cm), and serve.

COLONIAL RAISIN CAKES

At holiday time in the New England colonies, sweet biscuit-like cookies were baked on an iron skillet in the fireplace. This recipe was brought to America by settlers from the British Isles, where our celebration of Halloween originated. Trick-or-treaters will love these simple-to-make cookies, which, like their ancestors, can be baked in a skillet or frying pan. Eat them warm from the pan, spread with jam, or cool them and eat like regular cookies. Since you do not need an oven, this is a good project for a group of cooks to prepare in a club or classroom, baking on an electric skillet.

EQUIPMENT:
Electric skillet *or* frying pan
Large mixing bowl
Measuring cups and spoons
Metric scale—optional
Electric mixer *or* slotted spoon
Pastry board—optional; *or* wax paper
Rolling pin
Drinking glass *or* cookie cutters
Spatula *or* pancake turner
Wire rack
Serving platter *or* tray
Sifter

FOODS YOU WILL NEED:
1 cup (2 sticks) *plus* 1 tablespoon margarine *or* butter (255 ml; 255 g) at room temperature
¾ cup granulated sugar (185 ml; 165 g)
2 eggs
2 tablespoons milk (30 ml)
3 to 3¼ cups all-purpose flour (750 to 810 ml; 500 to 540 g)
1 teaspoon baking powder (5 ml)
½ teaspoon salt (2.5 ml)
¼ teaspoon cinnamon (1.2 ml)
¼ teaspoon ground nutmeg (1.2 ml)
½ cup seedless raisins *or* currants (125 ml; 80 g)
Jam *or* jelly and confectioners' sugar —optional

Ingredients:

(To make about 36 to 40 cookies 2½″ [6 cm] in diameter)

1 cup (2 sticks) margarine *or* butter (240 ml; 240 g)
¾ cup granulated sugar (185 ml; 165 g)

2 eggs
2 tablespoons milk (30 ml)

3 to 3¼ cups all-purpose flour (750 to 810 ml; 500 to 540 g)
1 teaspoon baking powder (5 ml)
½ teaspoon salt (2.5 ml)
¼ teaspoon cinnamon (1.2 ml)
¼ teaspoon ground nutmeg (1.2 ml)
½ cup seedless raisins *or* currants (125 ml; 80 g)

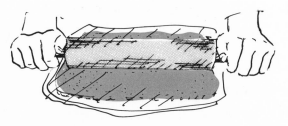

How To:

1. Set out electric skillet *or* frying pan, but do not turn heat on yet.

2. Use electric mixer *or* spoon to beat margarine *or* butter and sugar together in mixing bowl.

3. Break eggs into measuring cup 1 at a time, then add them to butter-sugar mixture in bowl. Add milk and beat well.

4. Measure just 3 cups (750 mg; 500 g) flour directly into bowl containing other ingredients. Add baking powder, salt, cinnamon, and nutmeg. Beat slowly until well blended. Add raisins or currants and mix well. Dough should feel stiff and form a ball easily. If needed, add more flour, 1 tablespoon (15 ml) at a time.

5. Turn electric skillet on to 375° F (190° C). Do not turn on stove yet if using a regular frying pan.

6. Roll out dough on lightly floured pastry board *or* wax paper (see Basic Skills). Roll dough about ⅛″ (0.25 cm) thick.

PRESS COOKIE CUTTER INTO DOUGH

CUT OUT COOKIE

1 tablespoon margarine *or* butter (15 ml)

Jam *or* jelly and confectioners' sugar—optional

7. If using frying pan, set it on stove now, over low heat to get warm. Dip rim of glass *or* edge of cookie cutter in flour sprinkled on wax paper, then press into dough, cutting rounds or other shapes. Peel away extra dough from between shapes.

8. Put about 1 tablespoon margarine *or* butter in preheated electric skillet *or* frying pan. Increase heat on stove to medium, if using frying pan.

9. Lift cut cookies with floured spatula *or* pancake turner and set them about 1″ (2.5 cm) apart on hot greased pan. Cook about 2 *or* 3 minutes on the first side, *or* until the cookie tops lose their shine and start to get firm around the edges. Turn cookies over and cook 2 *or* 3 minutes on other side, until browned.

10. Lift cookies out of pan with spatula *or* pancake turner and set them on wire rack to cool. Or, if you want to eat them warm, place them directly onto a plate, spread them with jam or jelly, and sift on some confectioners' sugar. If there are any cookies left, store them in an airtight container to keep them crisp.

COWBOY CRUNCH COOKIES

Made with chocolate bits, oats, and nuts, these crunchy cookies will quickly become everyone's favorite. So you'll be sure to have enough to go around, we've made this an extra-large recipe. If you like, you can freeze some of the dough to bake later.

EQUIPMENT:
Cookie sheets
Large mixing bowl
Measuring cups and spoons
Electric mixer *or* slotted spoon
Plastic bag *or* aluminum foil—optional
2 teaspoons
Timer
Potholders
Wire rack
Spatula

FOODS YOU WILL NEED:
1 cup (2 sticks) *plus* 2 tablespoons butter *or* margarine (270 ml; 270 g), at room temperature
¾ cup granulated sugar (185 ml; 165 g)
¾ cup packed dark brown sugar (185 ml; 200 g)
2 eggs
1½ teaspoons vanilla extract (7.5 ml)
2 cups all-purpose flour (500 ml; 325 g)
¼ cup wheat germ (60 ml; 30 g)
1 teaspoon baking soda (5 ml)
1 teaspoon salt (5 ml)
1 cup old-fashioned rolled oats (250 ml; 90 g)
1 cup chopped walnuts (250 ml; 125 g)
2 cups semisweet chocolate bits (500 ml; 350 g)

Ingredients:

(To make about 7 dozen cookies)

1 *or* 2 tablespoons butter *or* margarine (15 *or* 30 ml)

1 cup (2 sticks) butter *or* margarine (240 ml; 240 g), at room temperature

¾ cup granulated sugar (185 ml; 165 g)

¾ cup packed dark brown sugar (185 ml; 200 g)

How To:

1. Turn oven on to 350° F (175° C). Grease cookie sheets with butter *or* margarine.

2. With electric mixer *or* slotted spoon, beat butter and sugar together in mixing bowl.

2 eggs
1½ teaspoons vanilla extract
   (7.5 ml)

2 cups all-purpose flour (500
   ml; 325 g)
1 teaspoon baking soda (5 ml)
1 teaspoon salt (5 ml)

1 cup old-fashioned rolled oats
   (250 ml; 90 g)
¼ cup wheat germ (60 ml; 30 g)
1 cup chopped walnuts (250
   ml; 125 g)
2 cups semisweet chocolate
   bits (500 ml; 350 g)

3. Add eggs and vanilla to bowl
   and beat until ingredients are
   well blended.

4. Mix flour, baking soda, and salt
   into mixture in bowl. Stir slowly
   until well blended.

5. Add oats, wheat germ, nuts,
   and chocolate bits, stirring with
   large spoon until well blended.
   NOTE: You can freeze dough
   at this point by wrapping it in
   plastic bag *or* double-layered
   foil. Defrost dough before baking.

6. To make cookies, scoop up a
   heaping teaspoon of dough,
   then use second teaspoon to
   push it off onto greased cookie
   sheet. Place cookies at least
   1½" (4 cm) apart to allow room
   for spreading.

7. Place cookies in 350° F (175°
   C) oven. Set timer to bake
   cookies 10 minutes, *or* until
   golden around edges. Use
   potholders to remove sheet
   from oven and set on heat-
   proof surface. Lift slightly
   cooled cookies with spatula
   and set them to cool on wire
   rack.

PEANUT BUTTER–GRANOLA COOKIES

You can make your own Crunchy Granola Cereal (see index) or buy any variety of packaged granola in a grocery or health food store. Flavored with peanut butter and granola, these cookies are so good you will never notice that they are also very good *for* you!

EQUIPMENT:
Cookie sheet
Large and medium-sized mixing bowls
Measuring cups and spoons
Metric scale—optional
Electric mixer *or* slotted spoon
Wax paper
Sifter
2 teaspoons
Timer
Potholders
Wire rack
Spatula

FOODS YOU WILL NEED:
½ cup (1 stick) *plus* 2 tablespoons butter *or* margarine (150 ml; 150 g)
1 cup packed dark brown sugar (250 ml; 250 g) *or* light brown sugar (250 ml; 105 g)
1 egg
1 teaspoon vanilla extract (5 ml)
4 tablespoons milk (60 ml)
5 tablespoons peanut butter, crunchy *or* smooth type (75 ml)
1¼ cups all-purpose flour, sifted (310 ml; 170 g)
½ teaspoon baking soda (2.5 ml)
½ teaspoon salt (2.5 ml)
1 teaspoon cinnamon (5 ml)
1 teaspoon ground nutmeg (5 ml)
3 tablespoons wheat germ (45 ml)
2 cups crunchy granola cereal (500 ml; 185 g)
⅓ cup seedless raisins (80 ml; 55 g) *or* ⅓ cup chopped walnuts (80 ml; 45 g)

Ingredients:

(To make about 36 cookies)

1 *or* 2 tablespoons butter *or* margarine (15 or 30 ml)

½ cup (1 stick) butter *or* margarine (120 ml; 120 g)
1 cup packed dark brown sugar (250 ml; 250 g) *or* light brown sugar (250 ml; 105 g)

How To:

1. Turn oven on to 350° F (175° C). Grease cookie sheet with butter *or* margarine and set it aside.

2. Use electric mixer *or* slotted spoon to blend butter *or* margarine and sugar together in large bowl.

1 egg
1 teaspoon vanilla extract
(5 ml)
4 tablespoons milk (60 ml)
5 tablespoons peanut butter,
crunchy *or* smooth type
(75 ml)

1¼ cups all-purpose flour,
sifted (310 ml; 170 g)
½ teaspoon baking soda
(2.5 ml)
½ teaspoon salt (2.5 ml)

1 teaspoon cinnamon (5 ml)
1 teaspoon ground nutmeg
(5 ml)
3 tablespoons wheat germ
(45 ml)
2 cups crunchy granola cereal,
homemade (see index) *or*
store-bought (500 ml; 185 g)
⅓ cup seedless raisins (80 ml;
55 g) *or* ⅓ cup chopped
walnuts (80 ml; 45 g)

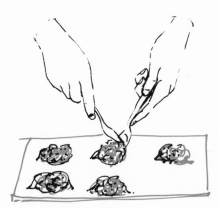

3. Break egg into measuring cup, then add it to butter-sugar mixture in bowl. Beat well. Then beat in vanilla, milk, and peanut butter.

4. Sift flour onto wax paper, then measure it and place in medium-sized bowl. Sift baking soda and salt into bowl over flour.

5. Spoon flour–baking soda–salt mixture into butter–sugar–egg mixture and beat very slowly until blended. Add cinnamon, nutmeg, wheat germ, granola, and raisins *or* nuts. Stir well with large spoon.

6. To make cookies, scoop up walnut-sized lumps of batter with 1 teaspoon. Use back side of second teaspoon to push batter off onto greased cookie sheet. Set cookies about 1″ (2.5 cm) apart so they have room to spread when baked.

7. Place cookies in 350° F (175° C) oven. Set timer to bake cookies 12 to 15 minutes, *or* until golden around edges. Remove pan from oven with potholders and set on heat-proof surface. Remove cookies from sheet with spatula while they are still warm. Cool them on wire rack.

SCOTCH SHORTBREAD

Shortbread, a super-rich sugar cookie, is quick and easy to make. Traditionally baked in the shape of a sun—a single large, round cookie—it can also be decorated to look like a jack-o'-lantern or cut with cookie cutters. In Scotland, shortbread is said to bring good luck and is often carried as a gift when you go visiting. Since Halloween is a time for fortune-telling, make lots of good-luck shortbread to share with trick-or-treaters. NOTE: Use only butter for the best flavor.

EQUIPMENT:
Measuring cups and spoons
Metric scale—optional
Large mixing bowl
Large fork *or* slotted spoon
Table fork, table knife
Cookie sheet
Rolling pin—optional
Cookie cutters—optional
Ruler
Timer
Potholders
Pancake turner
Airtight container

FOODS YOU WILL NEED:
1 cup (2 sticks) lightly salted butter (240 ml; 240 g), at room temperature
½ cup confectioners' sugar (125 ml; 65 g)
2 cups all-purpose flour (500 ml; 325 g)
¼ teaspoon ground nutmeg (1.2 ml)
2 to 3 tablespoons milk (30 to 45 ml)—optional

Ingredients:

(To make 1 round cookie about 8" × ½" [20 × 1 cm], which divides into 8 large wedge-shaped cookies or about 42 round cookies 2" (5 cm) in diameter

1 cup (2 sticks) lightly salted butter (240 ml; 240 g), at room temperature
½ cup confectioners' sugar (125 ml; 65 g)

How To:

1. Wash your hands, as you will be using them to mix and mold dough. Turn oven on to 325° F (165° C).

2. Measure butter into mixing bowl. Measure, then sift sugar into bowl. Blend butter and sugar together with your hands *or* with fork.

2 cups all-purpose flour (500 ml; 325 g)
¼ teaspoon ground nutmeg (1.2 ml)
2 to 3 tablespoons milk (30 to 45 ml)—if necessary

3. Measure, then sift flour directly into bowl over butter-sugar mixture. Add nutmeg. Use your hands *or* slotted spoon to work flour into the dough until it is all crumbly and flour is blended in. Do not overwork dough, or it won't be tender. Dough should now form a ball. If it is too dry to hold ball shape, sprinkle on 2 *or* 3 tablespoons (30 *or* 45 ml) milk and work it into the dough until easy to handle.

4. To make a traditionally shaped shortbread, gather up ball of dough and place it on *ungreased* cookie sheet. Flour your hands, then pat dough into a flat, round cake about 8" (20 cm) across and ½" to ¾" (1.5 to 2 cm) thick. Check size with ruler.

5. Use knife tip to cut scallops *or* notches around the outer edge of the circle; this makes the "sun's rays." Use the tines of the fork to prick lines dividing the cake into 8 equal-sized wedges, as shown. These lines should go through the thickness of the dough.

6. To vary the basic sun shape, you can use the cut-out dough scraps to make eyes, nose, and mouth shapes to add to the round sun face. Put a tiny dab of water under each bit of dough before pressing it in place. *Or* make a jack-o'-lantern. Leave the outer edge of the round cake smooth and cut away eyes, nose, and mouth with the tip of the knife, as shown. Make pumpkin stem with scraps of dough. *Or* roll out dough a scant ¼" (0.5 cm) thick and cut any shapes you like with cookie cutter.

WEDGE

7. Place pan in oven and set timer. Bake a whole single round piece of shortbread at 325° F (165° C) about 35 to 45 minutes, *or* until cake is golden around edges. Small cookies will take about 10 minutes. Remove pan from oven with potholders and set on heat-proof surface. When cold, use pancake turner to remove shortbread from the sheet. Break *or* cut whole shortbread into divided wedges. Store in airtight container. It is not very likely, but if shortbread should be around long enough to get soggy, it can be re-crisped in a warm oven for about 10 minutes. It is not traditional, but cakes can be trimmed with Decorative *or* Cream Cheese Frosting (see index) if you like.

HALLOWEEN NUT BALLS

In England and Scotland, so many Halloween (All Hallow's Eve) games and foods have to do with nuts that the holiday is often called "Nut Crack Night." These cookies, made with chopped nuts and rolled in powdered sugar, are popular holiday treats in the British Isles as well as around the world. In each country they have a different name, but they are always called *delicious.* They taste best made with sweet butter, but lightly salted butter *or* margarine will work, too.

EQUIPMENT:
Cookie sheet
Large and small mixing bowls
Measuring cups and spoons
Metric scale—optional
Wax paper
Sifter
Large spoon
Electric mixer *or* slotted spoon
Timer
Large platter *or* tray—optional
Potholders
Spatula *or* pancake turner
Airtight tin *or* cookie jar

FOODS YOU WILL NEED:
1 cup (2 sticks) *plus* 2 tablespoons sweet butter (270 ml; 270 g), at room temperature
2½ cups confectioners' sugar, sifted (625 ml; 250 g)
1 teaspoon vanilla extract (5 ml)
¼ teaspoon almond extract (1.2 ml)
2½ cups all-purpose flour, sifted (625 ml; 340 g)
½ teaspoon salt (2.5 ml)
1 cup finely chopped walnuts (250 ml; 125 g), *or* pecans *or* almonds

Ingredients:

(To make 40 to 45 cookies)

1 *or* 2 tablespoons butter *or* margarine (15 to 30 ml)

1 cup (2 sticks) butter *or* margarine (240 ml; 240 g), at room temperature

½ cup confectioners' sugar, sifted (125 ml; 50 g)

1 teaspoon vanilla extract (5 ml)
¼ teaspoon almond extract (1.2 ml)

2½ cups all-purpose flour, sifted (625 ml; 340 g)
½ teaspoon salt (2.5 ml)
1 cup finely chopped walnuts (250 ml; 125 g), *or* pecans *or* almonds

2 cups confectioners' sugar (500 ml; 200 g)

How To:

1. Turn oven on to 350° F (175° C). Wash your hands. Grease cookie sheets with butter *or* margarine and set them aside.

2. Measure butter *or* margarine into large bowl and press it into small pieces with spoon.

3. Sift confectioners' sugar onto wax paper (see Basic Skills), then measure and add it to butter. Use electric mixer *or* spoon to beat them together until smooth.

4. Add vanilla and almond extracts to butter-sugar mixture and beat well.

5. Sift flour onto wax paper (see Basic Skills), then measure and add it to other ingredients in bowl. Add salt and mix well. Stir in nuts.

6. Sift about 2 cups confectioners' sugar into small bowl and set it aside.

7. Flour your hands, then pick up small lumps of dough and roll them between your palms, making balls about 1″ (2.5 cm) in diameter. Set balls about 1″ (2.5 cm) apart on greased cookie sheets.

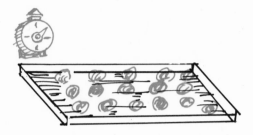

8. Set timer to bake cookies 10 to 12 minutes in 350° F (175° C), oven *or* until just golden around the edges. Use pot-holders to remove cookie sheet from oven. Place it on heat-proof surface.

9. Cut a sheet of wax paper approximately 14″ (36 cm) long and set it on a large platter *or* tray. Beside it place the bowl of sifted sugar.

10. Let cookies cool a couple of minutes, until you can comfortably touch them, though still warm. Use spatula *or* pancake turner to loosen cookies from the sheet.

11. Pick each warm cookie up in turn and roll it in the sifted confectioners' sugar in the bowl. Then set cookies on wax paper to cool completely. When they are cold, roll cookies in sugar a second time. Store them in an airtight tin, sprinkling them with more confectioners' sugar.

PECAN PIE

Everyone loves this traditional Southern specialty. It is surprisingly easy to prepare and is a good project for several cooks to work on together.

EQUIPMENT:

9″ pie plate
Wax paper
Pencil and scissors
Large mixing bowl
Measuring cups and spoons
Metric scale—optional
Pastry blender *or* 2 table knives
Dinner fork
Pastry board—optional
Rolling pin
Timer
Potholders
Small frying pan *or* saucepan
Wire whisk *or* eggbeater

FOODS YOU WILL NEED
(for pie crust *and* filling):

¾ cup (1½ sticks) butter *or* margarine (180 ml; 180 g)

1 cup all-purpose flour (250 ml; 165 g) *or* ½ cup all-purpose flour (125 ml; 80 g) *and* ½ cup whole wheat pastry flour (125 ml; 60 g)
2 tablespoons wheat germ (30 ml)
¾ teaspoon salt (4 ml)
3 tablespoons ice water (45 ml)
1 cup uncooked rice (250 ml; 200 g) *or* dry beans
¾ cup packed dark brown sugar (185 ml; 200 g)
3 eggs
⅔ cup dark corn syrup (160 ml)
1 tablespoon molasses, preferably unsulfured type (15 ml)
1 teaspoon vanilla extract (5 ml)
1 cup pecans without shells, halved (250 ml; 115 g)

Ingredients:

(To make one 9″ pie)

6 tablespoons butter *or* margarine (90 ml; 90 g)
1 cup all-purpose flour (250 ml; 165 g) *or* ½ cup all-purpose flour (125 ml; 80 g) *and* ½ cup whole wheat pastry flour (125 ml; 60 g)
2 tablespoons wheat germ (30 ml)
½ teaspoon salt (2.5 ml)
About 3 tablespoons ice water (45 ml)

How To:

1. Turn oven on to 400° F (205° C). Set pie plate face down on a piece of wax paper and draw around it with pencil. Cut out paper circle and set it aside.

To Make Piecrust

2. In mixing bowl, measure butter *or* margarine, flour, wheat germ, salt, and water. Work ingredients together with pastry blender *or* fork *or* 2 knives cross-cutting against each other until dough is cut up into pea-sized pieces.

3. Wash your hands, then use them to mold dough into a ball. Work in about 1 more table-spoon of water if dough feels too dry and crumbly.

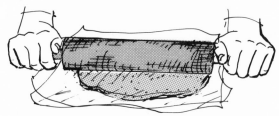

4. Roll out dough on lightly floured pastry board *or* be-tween 2 sheets of wax paper (see Basic Skills). Roll dough into a circle slightly larger around than your cut circle of wax paper.

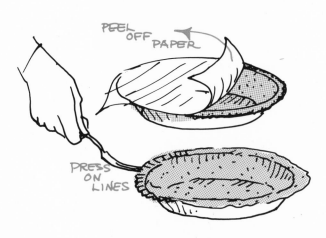

5. If you have used a top layer of wax paper while rolling dough, peel it off. Turn crust over onto the pie plate (peel off second paper), then gently press dough onto bottom and sides of pan.

6. To make a neat edge, pinch dough into an even-sized lip all around edge of pan. Then press tines of dinner fork into the lip all around, making lined pattern, as shown.

1 cup uncooked rice *or* dry beans (250 ml; 200 g)

7. To keep bottom of crust flat while it is baking, cover it with your wax-paper circle, then sprinkle rice or beans evenly over top. Set pan in oven. Set timer to bake 8 minutes at 400° F (205° C). Crust will bake more later, after it is filled. Use potholders to remove pie plate from oven. Leave oven heat on.

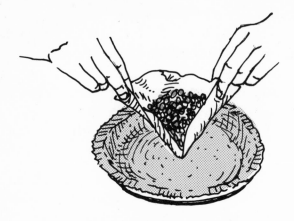

6 tablespoons butter *or* margarine (90 ml; 90 g)
¾ cup packed dark brown sugar (185 ml; 200 g)

3 eggs
⅔ cup dark corn syrup (160 ml)
1 tablespoon molasses (15 ml)
1 teaspoon vanilla extract (5 ml)
¼ teaspoon salt (1.2 ml)

1 cup halved pecans (250 ml; 115 g)

8. Cool pan on heat-proof surface. Then lift up edges of paper circle and carefully remove it from crust with the rice or beans inside. These can be saved and reused in the same way. Pick out any rice or beans that spill onto crust.

To Make Filling

9. Measure butter *or* margarine into small frying pan *or* saucepan and set on stove over low heat to melt. Wash and dry mixing bowl from crust-making. Pour melted butter *or* margarine into bowl. Beat it together with brown sugar, using spoon *or* whisk.

10. Add eggs, corn syrup, molasses, vanilla, and salt. Beat well.

11. Be sure there are no dry beans or grains of rice in pie shell. Then spoon *or* pour filling mixture into crust. Sprinkle nuts evenly over top. Place pie in 400° F (205° C) oven and set timer to bake 20 to 25 minutes. To test for doneness, stick knife blade into filling near *side* of pan; blade should come out clean if pie is done (filling may still be slightly soft in center). Use potholders to remove pie from oven.

CARROT CAKE

This nutritious, easy-to-make cake comes from northern Vermont, but an identical version is said to be a specialty of Costa Rica —proving that, wherever it is tasted, its moist texture and not-too-sweet flavor are quickly adopted and loved. Serve it plain, or with the Cream Cheese Frosting recipe that follows. Freeze plain *or* frosted cake wrapped in airtight foil *or* plastic.

EQUIPMENT

9″ (23 cm) ring *or* loaf pan *or* single layer
    cake pan
Vegetable peeler
Grater *or* blender
Paring knife
Rubber scraper
Measuring cups and spoons
Metric scale—optional
Large and small mixing bowls
Electric mixer *or* wire whisk *or* mixing
    spoon
Large spoon
Sifter
Timer
Toothpick *or* cake tester
Potholders
Table knife
Dinner plate
Wire rack

FOODS YOU WILL NEED:

1 tablespoon margarine *or* butter (15 ml)
1 cup *plus* 2 tablespoons all-purpose flour
    (280 ml; 185 g)
4 to 5 medium-sized raw carrots
2 eggs
1 cup granulated sugar (250 ml; 210 g)
¾ cup vegetable oil (185 ml)
3 teaspoons vanilla extract (45 ml)
1 teaspoon cinnamon (5 ml)
½ teaspoon ground nutmeg (2.5 ml)
1 teaspoon baking soda (5 ml)
½ teaspoon salt (2.5 ml)
1½ tablespoons wheat germ (25 ml)
½ cup chopped walnuts (125 ml; 65 g)

Ingredients:

(To make one 9" [23 cm] ring or loaf or single-layer cake)

1 tablespoon margarine *or* butter (15 ml)

2 tablespoons all-purpose flour (30 ml; 20 g)

4 to 5 medium-sized raw carrots

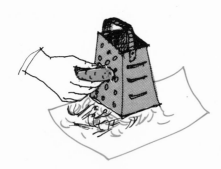

2 eggs

1 cup granulated sugar (250 ml; 210 g)

¾ cup vegetable oil (185 ml)

3 teaspoons vanilla extract (45 ml)

1 teaspoon cinnamon (5 ml)

½ teaspoon ground nutmeg (2.5 ml)

How To:

1. Turn oven on to 350° F (175° C). Grease pan with margarine *or* butter, then sprinkle inside of pan with flour. Turn pan over and shake out extra flour. Set pan aside.

2. Wash and peel carrots. Then grate them on large holes of grater, *or* cut them into small pieces and put about ¼ cup (60 ml) at a time into the blender. Blend 3 or 4 seconds, then turn off and *remove container from motor base.* Use rubber scraper to push cut carrots out into bowl. Repeat. Be sure there are no chunks larger than ¼" (0.5 cm). Place prepared carrots in measuring cup. You should have about 1½ cups (375 ml) when packed down firmly. Set carrots aside in small bowl.

3. With electric mixer *or* wire whisk *or* spoon, beat eggs and sugar together in large mixing bowl. Add oil, vanilla, cinnamon, and nutmeg, and beat again.

1 cup all-purpose flour (250 ml; 165 g)
1 teaspoon baking soda (5 ml)
½ teaspoon salt (2.5 ml)

1½ tablespoons wheat germ (25 ml)
½ cup chopped walnuts (125 ml; 65 g)

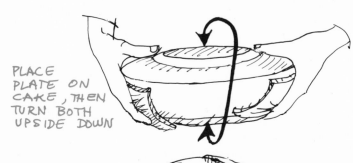

PLACE PLATE ON CAKE, THEN TURN BOTH UPSIDE DOWN

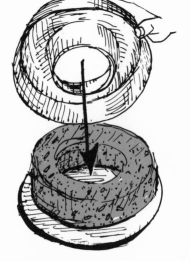

TAP, THEN LIFT OFF PAN

4. Measure flour, then sift it directly into bowl over egg-sugar mixture. Sift in baking soda and salt. Stir slowly until well blended.

5. Add grated carrots to mixture in large bowl. Then add wheat germ and nuts and beat together well.

6. Spoon batter into greased and floured pan. Clean bowl sides with rubber scraper. Place pan in 350° F (175° C) oven and set timer to bake for 40 to 45 minutes. Cake is done when toothpick stuck in center of cake comes out clean. Remove pan from oven with potholders. Set on heat-proof surface. Cool cake about 15 minutes before removing it from pan; to do this, slide a table knife between cake and side edges of pan to loosen it, then turn cake upside down over a plate and lightly tap bottom until cake falls out. Serve cake plain *or* with Cream Cheese Frosting, which follows. Baked in a round pan, the Carrot Cake can be decorated like a jack-o'-lantern.

CREAM CHEESE FROSTING

You can use this frosting plain *or* tint it to decorate a round jack-o'-lantern Carrot Cake (see index).

EQUIPMENT:
Measuring cups and spoons
Metric scale—optional
Electric mixer *or* slotted spoon
Sifter
Large mixing bowl
Rubber scraper
Table knife
Decorating tube—optional

FOODS YOU WILL NEED:
4 ounces cream cheese—½ a large package (125 ml; 115 g), at room temperature
4 tablespoons butter (60 ml; 60 g), at room temperature
1 teaspoon vanilla extract (5 ml)
2 cups confectioners' sugar (500 ml; 250 g)
Canned beet juice—optional
Frozen concentrated orange juice —optional
Baker's cocoa—optional

Ingredients:

How To:

(To make enough frosting for one 9″ [23 cm] ring, or a single layer or loaf)

4 ounces cream cheese—½ a large package (125 ml; 115 g), at room temperature

4 tablespoons butter (60 ml; 60 g), at room temperature

1 teaspoon vanilla extract (5 ml)

2 cups confectioners' sugar (500 ml; 250 g)

1. With mixer *or* spoon, blend cream cheese and butter together until smooth. Add vanilla and beat again.

2. Measure sugar, then sift it directly onto butter–cream cheese mixture in bowl. Beat slowly until combined and smooth. The longer you beat, the softer the frosting will get.

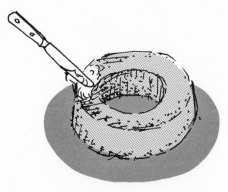

Few drops of canned beet
    juice—optional
1 *or* 2 tablespoons frozen con-
    centrated orange juice (15 *or*
    30 ml)—optional
1 tablespoon Baker's cocoa
    (15 ml)—optional

3. When frosting is smooth and
    soft, spread it over your cooled
    cake with a table knife.

    To decorate a jack-o'-lantern
cake, tint about ⅔ of the frosting orange. For color use a
couple of drops of canned beet
juice mixed with a tablespoon
or 2 of frozen orange juice.
Add extra confectioners' sugar
if frosting gets too soft after
coloring. In another bowl, add
a tablespoon of Baker's cocoa
to the remaining frosting to
make chocolate brown for
eyes, nose, and mouth. Draw
designs with decorating tube.

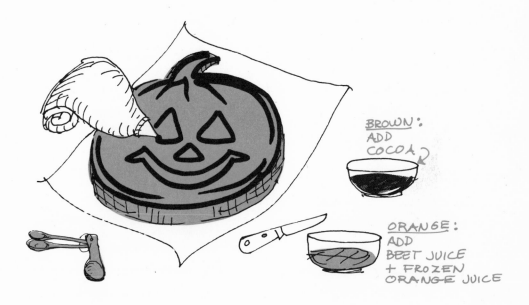

BROWN:
ADD
COCOA

ORANGE:
ADD
BEET JUICE
+ FROZEN
ORANGE JUICE

Index